AF492350

LUDOVICO

LUDOVICO

WILLIAM CASTANO-BEDOYA

BOOK&BILIAS

Coral Gables

For permissions, please contact Book&Bilias at
literaryworld@bookandbilias.us

ISBN 979-8-9888671-2-8 (Paperback English Version)
ISBN 979-8-9888671-3-5 (hardcover English Version)
ISBN 979-8-9888671-4-2 (e-book English Version)

ISBN 978-1-7369168-4-1 (Paperback Spanish Version)
ISBN 978-1-7369168-5-8 (hardcover Spanish Version)
ISBN 978-1-7369168-6-5 (e-book Spanish Version)
ISBN 978-1-7369168-7-2 (audiobook Spanish Version)

Library of Congress Cataloging-in-Publication Data available from the United States Library of Congress

General Direction: Camila Castaño
Writing and Editing: William Castaño-Bedoya
Cover Image and Layout: Book&Bilias

Printed in the United States of America

Book&Bilias
www.bookandbilias.us

To the Ludovicos who inspire me.

To those who care for and love them.

Happiness is what I like and can't be eaten,
can't be seen, but can be felt inside,
and it makes you say or not say but think that...

—I lo-o-ove it...
—This is-s so-o-o kool.

Ludovico Zonda

Table of Contents

In the exclusive streets of Coral Gables, Florida, USA, and amid the hidden corners of Medellín, Colombia, where everyday life pulses with its own rhythm, Ludovico's world unfolds—a conundrum of brilliance and naivety wrapped in layers of contradiction. He is a man in his forties, yet his mind bears the delicate innocence of infancy, a juxtaposition that defines his essence.

Ludovico's libido transcends mere physicality, entwining sensation and profound psychological perceptions. However, it is just one thread in the intricate tapestry of his experiences—a dance of complexities that defies conventional boundaries. To understand Ludovico is to embrace this nuanced fusion, to perceive the intricacies of desire through the lens of a childlike mind in an adult body. This novel delves into a myriad of themes, of which Ludovico's libido is just a single, albeit significant, exploration.

I invite you on a journey beyond the ordinary, a shared exploration of the human soul's mysteries. Ludovico is more than a character; he is a testament to the intricacies of the human mind. His apraxias, barriers to conventional communication, become windows into his soul—portals guiding you into his rich, unspoken world. Within these barriers lie whispered secrets, fears, desires, and aspirations, each revealing a profound depth.

His interior monologues echo through the chambers of his mind, forming a silent masterpiece of emotions. They are veins carrying the lifeblood of his narrative, inviting you to step into the vast landscapes of his thoughts. To read Ludovico's interior monologues is to embrace the unconventional, to journey with patience and sensitivity through the unspoken.

As we embark on this literary odyssey together, let your perception be as nuanced as Ludovico's desires, for within this complexity lies the heart of his narrative. Together, we will unravel, understand, and embrace his enigmatic world. Welcome to Ludovico's world, where the ordinary meets the extraordinary, where the mind's intricacies invite you to explore, empathize, and, above all, feel.

Author's Note

This character is inspired by wonderful individuals who have lived with Fragile X syndrome into adulthood. However, the situations described in the monologues have been conceived solely from a literary perspective.

From the First Day

"Wha-at the hee-ellll?" ?" I exclaimed.

It was all I could say when the plane touched down in Miami and jolted as if it were falling apart, rolling and rolling, very, very fast on the ground, battling against the gusty, harassing wind, angry that the plane had arrived without asking for permission and without intending to stop.

We were in that plane, making an effort to help it slow down or move more slowly, pushing against the furious wind that howled and shrieked because the plane wanted to beat it. Oh… I had a strong urge to pee, and I clenched my buttocks and squeezed my knees together to avoid doing it, just as my old lady tells me to do when I'm far from a bathroom.

I continued anxiously, feeling that the plane wouldn't stop because it was challenging the wind. I started sweating and sweating, and my armpits itched, and I had to scratch them until I felt lighter, without so much weight on my neck. I don't usually sweat much, just a little when I get overheated from the runs I take in Comuna Trece or when I'm overwhelmed by the feeling that I get when things don't go the way I want them to, and I lose control, and that feeling only goes away when I go to see the Baby Jesus in Santa Gema's church. I start feeling like the plane and the wind, tired of fighting each other, no longer want to make so much effort, and both think they've won.

Phew... Afterward, everything was calmer because the wind and the plane fell silent. People didn't look scared anymore, and my old lady kept looking at me with a smile in her eyes, though not on her mouth, as if she wanted to say, 'Calm down, my boy, we're still alive.'

We arrived a few lines before seven on my watch, which means the long hand pointed to the upper line, just like on my brother-in-law's watch in Miami, or to the dot on Amparo's watch, or to twelve on the wall clock in my house in Medellín, or my dad's, or almost seven, like my old lady taught me to say when someone asked me or whenever I felt like finding out the time. The lines thing is something I've known since the time when clocks actually had lines. I think I got used to seeing lines, even now when clocks don't have them or even if they have fake lines.

I thought we would arrive at seven, as my dad told me, but it seemed like the person piloting the plane decided to run or fly faster, like some big birds do to avoid being pecked by smaller ones that try to scare them away from the nests where their chicks are waiting for worms, flies, or bits of food, although I didn't see any small plane pecking at this one. I thought about it to understand it better. Anyway, that man who was piloting made the plane arrive faster.

I knew, because the plane stopped completely and some people applauded that we had avoided falling into the sea or the mountains or among the trees. My fear faded away when I remembered that I had traveled to avoid being alone in Medellín, looking from the terrace at the same things I see every day when people pass by, cars pass by, birds pass by. Everyone, except lizards, since there aren't any in Medellín, only in Miami. I'll see them when I get to Eleonora's house after they pick us up today. I'll see them, and they'll help distract me when I'm not distracted or when I'm in those days when nothing seems beautiful to me. There are days when I feel like nothing seems beautiful to me, but I'll remember that later because right now, I just want to remember what I'm thinking.

With me, they traveled, the usual ones: old Oslo, my dad, still asleep. That old man became calmer as he got older, but he used to be restless when he wasn't old yet and worked, and old Anastasia, my mom, who never sleeps during travels and also gets scared when we board the plane and when we arrive, and the plane fights with the wind.

We've been together for about forty-four years since I was born to them. The two of them have been together for much longer, much longer, something like since Igor was born, the oldest of all my siblings, who doesn't talk to my parents as if he had them punished. I felt joy, and I think so did they when the sound of unbuckling seat belts resembled the croaking of frogs as they gather to make chirping sounds on dark nights in the farms near Medellín. We sat waiting for the younger ones to take the lead and leave the plane empty. That's what we always do when we travel. My parents prefer it so as not to inconvenience people with the clumsiness the three of us are used to having. The three of us are very clumsy. I mean, when my mom tried to get up from where she was sitting, her heavy, round body sent her back to the seat. I offered myself as support, trying to help her lift her buttocks, but it was useless. They were too heavy for me, and my hands ended up underneath them. Then, my old lady got angry and rejected me, making a face that reminded me of how foolish I am. When she reminds me with her faces of how foolish I am, I remember that my face is different from other people's. For example, my eyes move like a dog's tail when it's happy, and other people's eyes don't. Maybe I'm stupid because my face is weird? My mother makes those faces at me, but I don't mind because I know she loves me more than anyone in this world. She makes faces at me playfully, trying to tell me to do things better, or... trying to say that I didn't do things right, but letting me know that ultimately it's not my fault and that the blame for her heavy buttocks lies solely with her and not me. Anyway, I took the opportunity when she moved and took my hands out from under her butt. I got confused trying to help her again, remembering when, a few weeks earlier, she fell in the garden because... supposedly she felt a lightning strike on her head, and she ended up asleep in the hospital, as my dad told me.

"How strange that she felt a lightning strike because that day it didn't even drizzle. Yes... how strange that because of a lightning strike, she ended up lying on the ground in the garden, smeared with mud on her back and with her arms scratched by the roses' thorns that she herself had planted for so long."

I cried in my bed alone that day. I cried because I've always had her close and smiling, or angry, or sad, or silent, as she always is when there's nothing to distract her, or whistling an old song when she remembers who knows what or when. I'd like to whistle, but I've never been able to learn. Whistling is too hard for me. Impossible, I would say. Every time I try, the wind comes out with drool, nothing more. When I want to whistle, I have to ask my mother to whistle for me, and then I listen to her quietly and thank her when she finishes whistling. She asks me if I want her to whistle again. Sometimes I ask her not to whistle whatever she wants but something I like, and she does it. Sometimes, when she's alone, she whistles things I like, even if I haven't asked her. I'm sure she thinks she can whistle to distract both of us at the same time.

Not every time does my mother want to whistle because she's tired or distracted by other things that have nothing to do with it.

My mother that day fell to the ground and kept

going, grumbling, as if leaving us, as if she didn't want to open her eyes anymore to keep seeing us—me, the turtledoves, the dog, and my old man. Since I know I'm me, I've never been alone when they travel because they never do it without me, and even though I felt fear and sadness for my mom that day, I calmed down when my dad made me understand that she would be fine after leaving the hospital. My mom is brave, but she's old now. She's been around for so many years that I can't count, something like eighty-two or maybe more, like two or three. My dad, on the other hand, is a few years older than her. The old man, unlike my mother, never worries about anything since he never has to do anything that's difficult. The heaviest thing he does is go for a walk every day, well-dressed, as if he were going to meet someone or as if someone were going to meet him. My mother, on the other hand, has to do everything in the house, from cooking for those who have arrived, to taking me to the doctor when I need to go or even taking herself when she feels something is going to hurt or has been hurting for days.

My mom's name is Anastasia, but I call her mom. She's the one who prepares my and my dad's clothes; she's also the one who changes my bed every Sunday. That old lady taught me to bathe every day. Because, yes, I bathe every day before going out and I wash my mouth with dental floss and a toothbrush after lunch and dinner. ... Ah! I also wash them when I wake up and when I go to bed.

My mother is as old as everything thrown in

the trash, but that still works. Poor thing, she became old taking care of me all the time. Thinking about my mom, I got distracted, forgetting that she wanted to leave already because the plane was completely empty. So, I turned my head to look at her again, and I saw her trying to get up from her seat again, with her little hands gripping the front seat, and when she finally managed to do it, I was the one who didn't let her pass because I was sitting in the aisle seat, next to the plane's corridor. She was sitting in the middle. That's when she tried to pass still holding onto the front seat when I pulled my legs back, but she had to give up because her body was too heavy for her. So, angrily, she made me understand that I had obstructed her first and second attempts. I was left speechless because I had already made two mistakes in a row, and my mother was confused. So was I. I felt embarrassed for this new clumsiness and tried to conceal it, although I felt hot on my forehead and my head was a mess. Then I tried to release her by asking her something unrelated to what was happening:

"Dih-d wee get toh May-ah-mee?"

She replied yes, but at that very moment, I couldn't understand her, and I moved my ear closer to her. She repeated it loudly with a few extra words to make me understand:

"Yes, we arrived in Miami. Find your suitcase!"

And she pointed upwards where everyone placed their suitcases. I realized that ours should also be brought down, just like my dad's woven flat cap that he wears on his trips to Eleonora's house, my younger sister, but older than me. She offered to give it to me on this trip if I promised her to travel calmly without bothering my mom and without making my dad angry when he talks to me occasionally and I don't manage to understand him. I tried to get up with strength, but this time, the seatbelt pushed me back. My mom noticed the tug and exclaimed:

"The seatbelt!"

And she pointed at it too. When I realized, I unbuckled it, making the last cric of that day and remembering the frogs on the farms. The old man, drowsy like the lanterns in the tavern where he drinks aguardiente every week with Tello, sat up, and in seconds, we were walking through the plane toward the door where the ones who gave us Coca-Cola, orange juice, and apple juice were waiting for us.

"Thank you."

They thanked us with smiles and something more, which, oddly, I couldn't understand. My mom and I had our red blanket taken away from our hands, which they had given us for the cold. It seemed strange to me because on other trips, we had taken the blankets with us. We walked toward the aisle that awaited us like a green lizard that devours everything without chewing it and would take us to the place where the policemen check the documents with stern faces. That's how I remember it since the last time we traveled. I was worried about the five suitcases because I was afraid I wouldn't recognize them since all suitcases look the same to me. I feared not finding mine with the magazine of the new video game device that I would share with my sister Eleonora. She offered to give it to me on this trip if I promised her that I would travel calmly without upsetting my mom and without making my dad angry when he talks to me, and I don't manage to understand him.

My mom was walking with difficulty due to some pains that had appeared in her knees thirty years ago, so many that I can hardly count, and according to what she told me, they developed from standing to cook every day for my dad, my eight siblings, and even for herself. I've noticed her more than him because I see that I have to help her more often than my dad. Besides, she's the one who always carries the flat purse with the travel documents, like the tickets sent to us by Irina, my middle sister, the one from Bradenton.

Every time I accompany my mom, I'm very afraid that something will happen to her. Some men snatch purses from ladies and run away. I hope it's not the same in Miami; I don't think so from what I remember from other trips, but I still like to stay close to my mom's purse. That's what I think; I don't know what those who steal purses think when they see me taking care of my mom with this silly face, skinny as a soda straw, and with my disobedient eyes. One day, being with my old lady at the supermarket, I saw a man taking an old lady's purse. He took it without any remorse. He snatched it, even dragged her, and she fell to the ground. What a fright I had. The bus that was approaching to pick up a few people almost ran over her. How sorry I felt for that old lady. I saw blood on her face and a lot of sadness. I wanted to help her because I got very angry. My mom didn't let me; I was screaming in fear. She was afraid that if she stayed alone, someone would take her purse. At least that's what I thought in the middle of all that confusion. Nevertheless, I followed the man to kill him. Yes, I wanted to kill him because he was evil, but several people, including some very angry women, had already caught him, and they were kicking his ass, face, chest, arms. That guy was screaming in pain, but no one helped him, not even me, who also wanted to finish him and make him pay for his audacity, so I gave him a kick. I only gave him one because other people also wanted to kick him. I think they killed him, I'm not sure—hence I say I think. Maybe they threw him in the trash like old things that no longer work or that got damaged for some reason.

Due to all that moment, I was confused, crazy, out of control, or more nonsense than usual, with that stupid thing that sometimes happens to me and I can't overcome. I was like that for a while, I don't know if it was short or long. A good while, I would say. At least my old lady spoke to me gently and told me that she was afraid something bad might happen to me being out there with that stupidity on the street. She asked me to please be happy while we got home, where she would give me the pill for the stupidity and then she would take me to the Church of Santa Gema to pray so that the Baby Jesus would calm me down. Just remembering the old lady's face makes me want to kill that boy. That little old lady shouldn't go out alone to buy bananas, or coffee, or anything. It's good that the stupidity left me that day. I think it was because I felt bad for the old lady and because I saw that they returned her purse. I think that's why.

I was glad to see that those who accompanied us on the plane during the trip had gotten to the front of the line first, but it didn't help them at all because we caught up with them. I made fun of them because my parents are so old, and I'm so dumb, that one of the policemen put us at the front of the line. Some people in the line pretended not to see me and turned their heads the other way. Others, less envious, just smiled as if trying to tell us not to be embarrassed because they weren't in a hurry. I thought they all seemed as foolish as the zebras on TV that crowd together in a hurry to cross the river without even thinking that the crocodiles will eat them almost whole. I laughed at comparing them all, including the old folks and me, with the zebras on TV. At some point during one of the trips, my mom told me that airport police officers were serious and that smiling always helped, even though they never did. That's why I always showed my teeth. I brushed them eight times before the trip.

We stood in front of the place where the officers in uniforms ask for documents. My mom stepped forward over the yellow line, recovering from a lecture from my old man, and I stayed behind them. We remained silent, watching the officer so as not to be distracted when he asked us to move forward. This didn't last long because he called us, moving his four fingers as if he were fanning himself. My mom was the first to notice because she had stayed attentive and didn't hesitate to nudge me with her elbow to make me concentrate. She said, "Smile."

I always ended up thinking about understanding what she told me, but before I could try to bring my ears closer, she made a new smiling face that I eventually understood. I remember she made the same face at my dad too. I showed my teeth, but my dad just grumbled, raising his eyebrows as if he didn't care, and muttered under his breath, "If they don't let me in, I'll go back to Medellín, and the problem will be over."

We walked a few steps following my mom until we reached the front of the policeman. She placed the small book with her photograph on the counter, then my dad's, and before placing mine, she gestured towards me. The very serious officer looked at me, then took a longer look, stretching his mouth like some men do in movies, and then he smiled with my mom. When the officer looked at me, I showed my teeth without laughing because at that moment I didn't want to. I hardly ever laugh with someone if their face looks like a crocodile's, and since that day I was comparing myself to the zebras, so I couldn't laugh with him. After all, zebras never laugh when crocodiles want to eat them.

I think the tooth brushing and showing them to the officer was a good thing. It didn't take long. A uniformed lady, along with another officer, took us to a separate room where they asked us to undress. My dad and I were left in just our underwear. They looked at our entire bodies with their eyes and hands, also with devices that made beep beep sounds. My mom got scared. I knew because her face turned red. Somewhat like the faces of turkeys in December when they get drunk with brandy and make them run forcibly before they kill them. I remember she also sweated on her chin, as she always does when she's confused. I always sweat on my forehead, but very little, almost nothing. I wasn't surprised because I knew at that moment, my mother would take out a tissue from the plane to wipe her sweat several times. My dad got scared too because he kept opening and closing his eyes non-stop, while putting saliva on his lips making kissing sounds. This happens when he has brandy in his stomach. Especially when he goes out on Thursdays with Tello, his lifelong friend, who has gone blind in his old age, but as he's used to going to the store to drink brandy for so many years, he doesn't care much about his blindness and never gets lost, even if he's very drunk.

While we were in that small place, the policewoman asked me my name. I got defensive. I looked for my mom and said, *"I do-o-on't kno-o-ow s-s-speak E-English."* My mom helped me understand, explaining that she had spoken to me in Spanish—just like in Medellín—and that I had to tell her my name.

I assumed that all the policemen in Miami only spoke English even though I had come to Eleonora's house many times.

I offered my hand as my mom had taught me since I was as small as Eduardito, and she shook it firmly. So, I introduced myself:

"Nice-to-meet-yoo-oo-uu- uu... Luuu-dovi-co Zon-da, Kos-lo-v, Ca-n-di-aa-aaa-ani, Pe-ttt-roooov... Nice-to-meet-yoooouuuu."

My mom helped her understand my name because after hearing me, she seemed not to have understood. She looked at my face and made sure I was the same person in the small green book where my picture is always glued and it says what my name is and when I was born. Then she showed me a package of flour, the same one my mom uses to make elephant ears that I like so much in the soup we all call ear soup, and she asked me, "Where is the flour you brought?" I didn't understand at all because I didn't know what she was talking about. The package looked like a wrapped tamale, like the ones we buy when we go out to eat tamales in Medellín, those days when my mom doesn't want to cook because her ankles hurt or because she just doesn't feel like it. That's when I looked at my mother and asked her very puzzled, *"Fl-ooo-uur??? I-don't unn-der-stannn-d?"*

"It was very strange that she asked me about flour because we've never brought flour on any of our trips," I mused. My mother usually brings beans, fruit candies, coffee, and other things, but not that. My mother got very angry when that lady asked me, and she angrily said something like, "Do you think we're bringing cocaine or something? Shameless!"

I didn't understand and still don't. The lady didn't say anything; she pretended nothing happened, but my dad did. For the first time on that trip, my dad got weird, like when he doesn't like something. After a few minutes and already dressed, we left the place and walked alone through the halls. We were tired and didn't talk at all. Only my mom's breathing could be heard and the sounds from the speakers, just like at Medellín airport, but in English. It felt like minutes that seemed like hours or days. Finally, we managed to see my suitcase and my parents' four suitcases. They were scattered everywhere, but I think they were happy to see us. After all, they were the only ones left. I dragged them together and managed to pile them onto an airport trolley with some help from my dad, who sometimes pretended not to see them, and finally, we got out. That long way from the plane seemed to me again like the one the zebras on TV follow. After kicking and kicking, they reach the other side of the river, but because of the long wait, I thought we would become the zebras that can't make it and end up torn to pieces and eaten by the alligators.

It was so good to see them! Everyone my mom told me would come to greet us was there: Eleonora, her husband Tomás, and my little nephews Eduardito and Camila. I looked at my mom to tell her that I had already seen them, but I realized that she was already smiling at them just like my dad. It's very possible that they had seen them long before I did because I've never been quicker than them to find people. Truth be told, almost everyone sees things faster than I do, including my old folks. My eyes don't see the same way others do, nor do they see as quickly. Only one sees, the right one, because when I cover it with my hands, it's like when the light goes out just before I fall asleep. My good eye, my right eye, is glued behind the only window where the light enters me. And don't think it's a window as big as a house window. No. That window is very small. To give you an idea of how big it is, at most, a squirrel can fit through it crouched, and it fits with difficulty. The truth is, from there, I usually look at everything I need to look at. I mean, I look at everything I can see. Just so you know, that window is always open during the day when the light shows itself and I'm not asleep, or at night when there's a light bulb in front of it, like the lantern that lets me see the lizards, or even the moonlight when it resembles a lit bulb to me. That window is always in front of my right eye, my good eye, my friend.

Something I like about my right window is that it's always where I am. It's my friend, I've said it. We stay together, stuck together like fingers to my hands or like ears to my head, so you understand better. When I move, the window moves with me. It's not that it follows me like the little character in the video game who spends his time chasing the good guy who won't let himself be killed or the bad guy I have to chase and who I have to kill. No. It's as if I'm forced to chase that window everywhere it goes, and it's forced to chase me. In other words, everywhere I move my head when my eye is open, it moves too, and when it's closed, it is too. The truth is, I'm trying to tell you that my eye and the window are the same.

Once, when my mother took me to the eye doctor, when I was little, about thirteen years old, they said one of my eyes works, but it can only see straight ahead and not as much as other people can see around them. That is, my window isn't as big as Igor's or old Oslo's, or Irina's or Amparo's windows, which, among other things, are beautiful windows. They're beautiful, very beautiful, gorgeous; they're brown, without any heavy black curtain that prevents the entry or exit of light or seeing the wonderful things that pass through with the light. How does Amparo see me through her windows when I show up to greet her and say, *"He-he-hello, wha-a-at's up?"* or *"Wha-a-at's go-o-o-ing on?"*

Will she see myself the same way I see myself in the mirror? Maybe she'll see myself the same. Surely, her windows are not as troublesome as mine, which, due to their small and inconvenient size, don't allow me to stick my head out to see what's happening around me, above or below. My window is very annoying, but it's my window, and there's nothing I can do about it.

So, when I need to look to one side—for example, to my left—I have to align my gaze with the right side of my small window because its thick frames don't let me see to my left. From there, I make an effort to see. I don't know if I made myself clear. You must be as confused as old Oslo when he talks to me, and I don't understand a word. In other words, I will explain that, for me to be able to look sideways, I do the same thing prisoners do. Even if they want to see their friends in the neighboring cell, they can't because they can only look straight ahead. What a pity that prison cells don't have windows on the sides so that those inside can sit and talk, just like the people who work at the bank where my dad buys money. Those people hardly work because every time we go to the bank to buy money, we have to wait in lines while they chat and chat instead of selling the money to my dad without so much delay. Sometimes I think those working at the bank should be in prison to learn to look only straight ahead, at the people who need to buy money .

How much I wish sometimes to open my window, tear it open as if it were stuck to a paper wall, tear it until there's a hole as big as the windows my brothers have, or my few friends, or those who are not as much, like Amparo's little sister. If my window were as big as the windows of normal people, I would surely stick my head out of it and look wherever I wanted. But... there's nothing to be done. From what I've been able to understand, every time I ask, I've thought that people have two windows from which to look. Two windows as big as their house windows from where they can even go out or come in if they forgot their keys. I could be wrong. It's possible that they also have only one window like mine, and not two as big as I imagine. My small window is attached to a big black wall, and I don't know where it starts or where it ends.

Anyway, I was happy to be back in Miami because in Medellín, many of my friends or acquaintances are already dead due to bullets they found on their way or simply because they got old. I couldn't contain my happiness. So, I exploded, looking for my mom's face, saying:

"Da-da-da-amn it, w-w-we arr-r-rived in Mi-mi-miami, I-I-I do-don't w-want Me-me-Medellín anymore!"

Although we had already greeted each other with looks and smiles when we were still far away, Eleonora hugged my mom, and Tomás, her husband, hugged my dad. I waited my turn, as always when the three of us arrive somewhere together, that is, last. That's when Eleonora hugged me and kissed my cheek so loudly that it echoed throughout the airport. —"What's up, baby!" she said, gracing herself with a smile as big as her mouth.

I accepted her hug, but I couldn't help responding angrily, scolding her:

—*"I-I-I don't l-l-like being c-c-called B-b-baby; my n-n-name is L-l-ludovico. B-b-baby is l-l-little E-e-eduardo or l-l-little C-camila. I-I am a b-b-big man, v-v- very big. Pl-*

pl-please, n-n-never c-c-call me b-b-baby again, n-n-never again!"

Eleonora was amazed by my complaint. Sometimes I get angry unintentionally. She's the one who taught me the a, the e, the i... and to write words with a pencil. She also taught me to know the names of colors and to add simple things like one plus three, five plus eight, and other things I don't remember. How bad I was to get angry with Eleonora because she called me a baby. She didn't know I wasn't one anymore. Anyway, she's known me since I was little. Nevertheless, to make me not angry anymore, she promised me that she would never call me that again. I felt ashamed because I really like her. Somehow, I tried to change my attitude and looked for my mom with my eyes. She, who was always attentive to me, understood everything.

"Mo-mo-mother, t-t-tell El-eleonora to n-n-never call me B-b-baby again!"

As best as she could, amidst the greeting, my mom explained to Eleonora the reason for my anger. She let her know that although I've always liked being called a baby, now that I had met Amparo, I didn't want to be called that anymore. That's very true. Now I feel like a grown-up. As grown-up as those who already have a girlfriend. Amparo is beautiful. Her body is the prettiest in Medellín, Miami, Chicago, and the whole world. Including London, where Raisa lives. Amparo is prettier than all the women put together. Her arms, her face, and her legs are the color of leaves falling without being completely dry, not brown, like her very eyes. Her hair is as black as the darkness of my nights when I sleep without remembering her, and her smile, as big as my desire to see her every day.

"I l-l-love eer!" I told Eleonora when my mom told her about her.

Every time I go jogging around La Villa, or better... around Comuna Trece, my mom doesn't know, I can't help but stop to greet her. Once she was with one boyfriend, the other time with another. She always has new boyfriends, boyfriends with lots of money. Boyfriends who arrive in big, new, shiny cars. I remember her a lot. Her few years make her beautiful and happy. She always smiles. When I sleep, I see her hugging and kissing me like in the soap operas my mom watches on television or like in the movies I always watch when everyone is asleep. Sometimes, when I remember her while sleeping, I wet my pajamas, and I feel my mind shake just like my tutu, which straightens and straightens, and rises until it gets tired and becomes very small. When that happens, I wake up early the next day and go out to run just to see her and confirm that my thoughts while sleeping are real. When she sees me coming, if she's around, she greets me:

—"Hello Lu-do-vi-i-i-ico!" And I answer her:

"He-he-hello, wha-a-at's up?" or "Wha-a-at's go-o-o-ing on?"

She offers me water when I'm thirsty at her door.

When she's not around, someone offers me water, and if they don't, I ask for it, and they give it to me if they don't act dumb. They already know me and are fond of me. Especially those who don't act dumb when I ask for water. I was glad to know that Eleonora understood my anger and hugged me tightly, kissing me on the cheek. Anyway, she made fun of me because she called me a baby again.

I think she understood when I told her about Amparo as she asked me, while we were walking through another one of those hallways. Among other things, I tried to let her know about my sadness for not being able to see her that same afternoon. I also told her that sometimes she offers me drinks to quench my thirst and lends me napkins from the dining room to wipe off the little sweat that comes out of my body when I run all day. Anyway, now happy to be with them, I hugged her back. I felt happy to see part of my family together because for the last twenty years, the old folks and I have been waiting for the days to clear and darken in silence, scaring away the pigeons that come to the balcony of my house and shit on the railings.

We went looking for the airport parking lot after walking and walking through different hallways that connected to other parking lots. My brother-in-law went ahead to bring the car that would take us to his house where he now lived, and none of us knew. We finally arrived at a point where Eleonora led us. We could see that Tomás was already waiting for us with all the car doors open, including the back one. Recognizing that the car was the same as a few years ago, I didn't hesitate to express my comment:

"Tha-a-t ca-a-ar is ve-e-ry o-o-old!"

He understood my words and smiled. How good it is that since the day we first met, about ten years ago, during my family's trip to Miami for his wedding to my sister, my brother-in-law learned to understand my questions and comments without getting annoyed. He explained to me that, although he wanted to have a new car for my arrival, he hadn't been able to do so due to a lack of money. I didn't hesitate to suggest that he go to the bank to borrow money so he could have a new one. He smiled and promised me that he would buy one for my next visit. That was enough for me. My brother-in-law sweated as he carried the five suitcases upstairs. I helped him when he asked. It was very hot. We sweated and smiled at the same time. When we got into the car, we felt the coolness of the air conditioning, which was working and making a noise that forced us to talk loudly to hear each other. In just a few minutes, we managed to get on the highway heading home. In the car, three conversation groups formed. Eleonora and my mom on one side. My brother-in-law took care of talking to my dad, and it was my task to handle Eduardito and little Camila. When she saw my strange look so close to her, she began to cry, searching for Eleonora eagerly. She quickly calmed her down with the help of little Eduardo. After a few minutes, we arrived home. We were eager to see my sister's new home. My mom had told me that the beautiful house they used to have had been exchanged for this old, run-down house.

The first thing I noticed was that night came later in Miami, around eight o'clock. In Medellín, it arrives around six. Despite Eleonora's house being fit for the trash, smelling old, and with all the peeling walls, we imagined that it would be like new for our next visit. Although I was very happy to be there, I couldn't help but remember Amparo smiling. I think I missed her.

During the rest of the day, I played with the children. I made faces similar to those the street performers make at the traffic lights in Medellín, hoping for some coins. I did it to make them laugh a bit because they don't have any coins. I also wrote their names on a piece of paper and showed them. I wanted them to know that I could also write some words without Eleonora's help. Something that kept me entertained was watching so many new cars pass by the house.

My dad, my mom, Tomás, and I had dinner at a round table. The children sat in two small plastic seats, one blue and one red, next to a small white plastic table. Later, Eleonora dragged a chair and joined the group, and they chatted animatedly. When I saw them laughing a lot, I laughed too because I couldn't tell if they were laughing because of a very good joke or a really stupid one—like when an old person trips, falls, and someone laughs. What a pity for the old people when they trip. Since I was a child, I've gotten used to laughing when others do, and no matter how big their laughter is, mine must be doubly exaggerated. I think I am happy when everyone else is happy.

That night, I slept on the couch. I felt comfortable, maybe because I was so tired. When the whole house fell silent, and the lights dimmed to let us rest, I remembered some things. Like when we were naked together in the airport room or when I was still in Medellín, and I ran to Comuna to see Amparo smile and tell her that I would travel to Miami with my parents. That day I said to her:

"To-to-tomorrow Miami."

But she didn't understand, although I tried my best to make her. She is not as good at understanding my words as my mom or my siblings or my brother-in-law. However, I repeated it to her in various ways:

"I'm f-f-flying to M-M-Miami, m-m-mom, d-d-dad, s-s-suitcases, f-f-f-five in the m-m-morning."

I repeated it several times until she finally understood and asked me triumphantly:

"Are you going to Miami?!"

I said yes. She smiled and ruffled my hair. I like it when she does that.

Before falling asleep, I reviewed all the conversations I had heard during the day. I always do it, even though I don't understand everything I hear. And although I always hear everything they say, I am never part of the conversations. Speaking of that or something like that, I remember one day my mom was explaining to someone over the phone, someone I never knew who it was, that supposedly the doctor had told her that Ludovico, me, only understood ten percent of what he heard but understood everything his own way. That comment caught my attention because I heard my name. When I asked my mom, she didn't understand my question, and in the end, I had to swallow it. That ten percent thing has me very intrigued, that is, for me, it has always been a very big mystery. At this point, I still have that question stuck in my throat. To put it correctly, I never talk to them because I am slow to understand what they say. The truth is, when they talk to me, most of the time, I get lost. But I don't forget the words I hear. How much I would like to have a long conversation with someone. Well, I enjoy it more when they ask me for favors, and my mood is good. I think I never feel lazy to do it.

Unlike Eleonora's house, our house in Medellín is large and quiet. I mean, without noises. The few noises that are heard in the house are from the pots in the kitchen and the cooing of the doves nesting in the garden in the backyard. Sometimes, the noise of the telephone makes me react. It is always my mom who answers because they never call my dad and me. Well… almost never. Sometimes my mom shouts from the first floor:

"Ludoviiiiiiiiico, it's Hugo."

Hugo is my friend from Medellín. My mom refers

to him as a "slow idiot," well, she doesn't say it to me, but I hear her every time she says it to someone on the phone. I have never managed to understand what "slow idiot" means; I just know it means being stupid. When I remember, I will try to ask Eleonora. I will try to ask her, I will, but I don't know if she will realize that it is exactly what I want to ask her... we'll see.

Hugo always calls my house to tell me he is coming to visit me on the bicycle his mom bought for him in New York. What a pity that he doesn't know his mom, nor does he know New York because, as he tells my mom when they occasionally talk in the dining room while we have lunch, she left him when he was just a child supposedly to go to New York with a man who is not his dad. He also says that his grandmother tells him that she loves him very much, and that's why she sends him gifts like the bicycle and the device to play videos. Hugo is the same age as me, and he talks better than I do with others, although he is very slow in his movements and very fat. He eats a lot... he looks like an animal. I am fast when I move, but I can't speak well, and I don't understand everything. He is slow. It makes me sad because he doesn't have his mom, and I do. We play videos in silence. We couldn't do it while talking because we would lose the game. We hardly exchange words. I think we understand more from each other's faces, and that's why we don't talk.

My mom calls us to have guava juice or to eat. She is always attentive to Hugo and me. When Hugo is tired of playing videos, he goes home, and I am left alone, again playing or watching television until three in the morning.

I remember meeting Hugo once when they took me to study with other kids like me. It was a school for idiots, or rather, for stupid people. Some who don't know how to speak, including me, others who have stiff hands and neck, others who drool like babies, others who walk and talk slowly like Hugo, and others who shout and tremble. It was very bad to have studied with so many crazy people. Only Hugo remained calm. We became friends until we decided we didn't want to return one morning when a boy hit Teacher Matilde with a thick book. He hit her very hard because he was crazier than usual that day, yes… he was crazy. The teacher was scared and in pain. She almost fell from the pain. I was so angry, so much, that I was on top of that boy, hitting him. My mom told me that I bit his neck and shoulder and that I only let go when other teachers arrived. I bit a piece of his shoulder off with my teeth. He cried a lot and screamed, but I never let go. There was blood on his clothes, and his eyes were full of fear because of me. He will never hit Teacher Matilde again. That's what I think. That day, I didn't go back to school. I will never go back. And that's how I fell asleep on my first night in Miami, at Eleonora's house, with my brother-in-law and the kids.

One Day Later

When I woke up, around noon the next day, everything seemed like a mystery due to the profound silence. I even thought I was alone in a house that wasn't mine, and the whole trip felt like a movie you watch when you're asleep. Apparently, they had all agreed to let me sleep as long as my body wanted. Surely, they had already had breakfast. Thanks to them, my first morning was calm. I peeked through the blinds facing the street, and the sunlight glinted into my good eye, unaccustomed to darkness, but it encouraged me to get up. The first thing I remembered was something I heard the night before from everyone's lips, which intrigued me. According to them, my eight siblings would be arriving at this small house throughout the week. Where would we accommodate seven more people if even the couch was occupied by me? Artur would arrive from Chicago the same day. He has always lived there. He has a big, new truck. I think he'll bring me the catalog of his truck as a gift. He always does that whenever he buys a new one. Irina would also be arriving from Bradenton in her gray Volkswagen, the same color as my mom's pots, with a yellow flower next to the steering wheel.

Irina loves the color yellow. I think that color is sad… or not entirely sad. Perhaps her sadness isn't because of the color yellow but because that's how I see her. To me, she appears sad, even when she's laughing. I can see it in her eyes, hiding the sparkle of other eyes. The eyes of other people who are never, almost never, sad, or if they are, their sadness doesn't show in their gaze… that's what it seems like to me. It would be nice to see her Volkswagen. Her pot-colored Volkswagen, as she calls it herself. She sent me the catalog when she bought it new last year. I really like new cars. My siblings send me catalogs of their cars when they're new. I always keep them in my room, and when Hugo comes to visit, we look at them, provided we're not playing videos. Fausto, my other brother, older than Eleonora, will arrive two days later in his old car from Key West. What a pity Fausto doesn't have a new car. When he arrives, I'll ask Irina to buy him one or lend him her Volkswagen. I also understood that Raisa would be arriving from London. London… what a hassle… and Raisa, what a hassle. I was cold when I was in London. The day was gray all day. Anatoli will also be arriving from New York by plane, like us. I'll ask him if they made him undress like when we arrived from Medellín and if they also asked him if he was carrying flour. Eleonora explained to me that when Colombians arrive in Miami, the police think we all carry flour. They must really love making bread… Anatoli is the second oldest among my siblings, and he's the first one who came to the United States. Everyone at home says he has a lot of money but no new car. He has a lot of money, but it's saved, I think. Everything he has is old: his shoes, his car, his beds, his blankets, in short, everything he has, even his wife. Ah! He also has some new things like his friends from Medellín.

When Anatoli arrives in Medellín, he almost always comes alone, without his usual wife, Irma. He shows up at the house with new friends, meaning not as old as him. In that way, he's like me; I like Amparo, that beautiful girl I like so much. I like her also because I've never liked old things. When they took me to New York to visit Anatoli, we only traveled by train underground. New York scares me.

Igor, the oldest of all my siblings, will also be arriving this week from Medellín. My mom says, when she talks on the phone with her friend Cecilia, that Igor is very ill-tempered and doesn't have his own house. That's true. Besides, he also drives an old car that I don't like. I've heard many times that my dad has favored Igor more than the others because he's the oldest and because he accompanies him on Fridays to play billiards and drink aguardiente. Well, that was before, because my dad only goes out to drink on Thursdays with Tello. According to him, he's already too old, and he's forgetting how to play billiards. As for Boris, my older brother than me but younger than Fausto, we'll see him that same afternoon since he lives in another house in Miami, far from Eleonora's. What a drag to see Boris again. He's always drunk and talks non-stop, saying vulgar things. Anyway, I think they noticed I woke up because I heard voices and laughter. I walked to the kitchen where everyone greeted me almost in unison:

—*"Hello Lu-do-vi-i-i-ico!"*

"Wha-a-at's up?" I replied, drowsy and with my eyes still swollen and squinting.

My mom, with little Camila in her arms, was sitting in a round armchair, one of those wooden ones. Judging by the smell, they were preparing lunch. I confirmed it when I saw my mom wearing a flowery apron, just like Eleonora's. Whenever she gets up, she puts on an apron and only takes it off after serving us lunch and washing the dirty dishes. Sometimes, she takes it off earlier when I tell her I'll help her wash the dishes. I like washing dishes at home when I'm not busy, looking out over the terrace, seeing the same things I see every day. I also spotted my dad dozing off in the room visible from the kitchen. He always dozes off with the television on, at any time of the day and in any house he's in. Occasionally, when I wake up at 5 in the morning because I need to pee or before turning off my TV at 3 in the morning, I turn off his TV to let him snore peacefully.

"How did you sleep?" Eleonora asked.

"Ah, I s-s-s-lee-e-e-pt well," I replied, as I always do when everything is fine.

I looked at the microwave clock and knew it was already noon. I knew it because when it's past twelve, it means the afternoon is about to begin and the morning has ended. I felt a bit embarrassed to have woken up at this hour at Eleonora's house. People usually wake up in the morning. She noticed and spoke slowly to make it easier for me to understand:

"It's, until now, twelve o'clock, it doesn't matter… it's not late. Miami is nice! Don't be embarrassed."

"*Tha-a-a-nk you-u-u,*" I replied, grateful for her kindness.

She offered me breakfast, which was already prepared and stored in the same microwave where I saw the time, and which I had chosen as my favorite clock since the previous day. This clock doesn't have stripes but numbers. I think it's easier for me to see the time with numbers than with stripes. The children greeted me affectionately. I spent a few minutes with them while the table was set. Eleonora sat down to accompany me. Apparently, my brother-in-law was working. He always joins me at the table when I come to Miami. I took advantage of having Eleonora nearby and asked about my other siblings who would be meeting us:

"*When do-d-d-oes Irina, Bo-o-o-ris, Fa-a-a-usto, Artur, I-i-i-gor, R-ra-a-isa arrive? When?*"

She answered me the same as what I had heard the night before. They would arrive every day of the week. It made me happy, but I doubted it was Christmas in June. I remember that when all the brothers gathered with Mom and Dad, it was to give Christmas presents. I didn't hesitate to keep asking:

"Str-strange, eve-everyone in Mi-mi-Miami, the B-baby Jes-sus is in D-d-december!"

She clarified that it wasn't Christmas. They had planned to be together with Dad, Mom, and me, as they had been far away for many years, and we remained alone in Medellín. I felt relieved to hear that because every day, I hear my mom say that someone we know has died. It's strange, all the old folks die except those in my house. I also felt scared and sad when I thought about it, and I told Eleonora:

"I, ve-ve-very sa-a-a-ad."

"—Sad? Why? —" she asked curiously.

"Li-i-i-a di-e-e-ed, Jo-o-o-rge di-e-e-ed, Pa-a-a-tricia di-e-e-ed."

"—Don't be sad, baby. They died happy. They were old, very old —" she replied, hugging me affectionately.

I told her the only thing that came to mind when we were hugging:

"Wha-a-a-t a p-p-pity.."

"—Yes, what a pity —" she exclaimed.

She also asked me not to worry because, according to her, Mom and Dad were very relieved. She said they were so relieved that they would live to be a hundred. I know that from eighty to a hundred, there are twenty years. That means I'll have them for twenty more years. I asked her how old I would be by then. She said I would be old, with white hair like León, my mom's brother, who has white hair. I showed her that I already have some white hairs on my head.

It was three in the afternoon, and my brother-in-law should go to the airport to pick up Artur. I waited for him to invite me; he always does. That day was no exception. He didn't even ask me, just said:

"Let's go, Ludovico!"

Although I was waiting for his departure, I asked to be sure.

"Sh-shall we g-g-g-o? Wh-where to-o-o?"

"To the airport, for Artur."

"Ar-tur? Wha-a-a-t?"

"Yes... For Artur, to the airport, let's go!"

And we got into the white Cherokee Laredo, which I had known a few years earlier when he had picked us up at the airport the day before. It was clean because my brother-in-law had washed it early to make sure Artur found it perfect, just as we had found it when he picked us up at the airport. I noticed that despite being an old car, it was fast and comfortable. We engaged in conversation. He always asks me about things he doesn't understand when I talk about them. He pays a lot of attention to me; it seems like he genuinely cares about me, like one cares about friends. Just like I care about Hugo, who, although he's very slow, I always want to know what he wants or what he's saying, no matter if he says it with his eyes, words, or his gaze. With my brother-in-law, I talk about things I never talk about with anyone else. He's a friend I really care about, like Hugo. I tell him about the movies I watch on television. He laughs when he hears me say that women come out with their breasts exposed and always go to bed with men, shouting and shouting and pinching and pinching them, and sometimes two women come out with a man, and sometimes three or four, and I really like to see them get together and get together, and when I go to the supermarket with my mom, I see the pretty girls walking, and in my eyes, I see them without clothes, shouting and pinching me until they finally get tired of shouting and pinching me.

Sometimes when I go out with my mom, she scolds me because my pants are stretched over the tutu, so I think about other things, and it goes away. Other times, I don't feel anything because I don't feel like seeing them without clothes, pinching me, or shouting that day. It's fun. My brother-in-law tells me I'm mischievous. I always say I'm like the devil, very naughty. He tells me everything is fine and that it's not bad to see naked women because I'm over forty. He's a good brother-in-law. Sometimes he lets me have a beer without my mom noticing. He pours it into a glass as if it were for him and tells me I can drink when my mom isn't looking. I like to have a beer every Friday when I have Medellín money, not money from the United States. On that day, I pass by the bar where my dad and Igor play billiards and buy a beer. After I've had it, I go out to jog or walk because I feel a bit slow, but not thirsty. I'm already a grown-up and have a girlfriend. Grown-ups like me drink beer. I also told my brother-in-law about Amparo. He was happy for me and asked if I had a photo for him to see her, and I told him I didn't. I also told him that Jorge, a friend from Comuna Trece, had died. The police in Medellín killed him when he was in an expensive car. They also killed his girlfriend. He had a gun and killed a police officer before they killed him and his girlfriend. My brother-in-law asked how I knew about that, and I told him I saw it one day when I went to see Amparo, but I hid in her house. I remember she told me in a hurry, almost dragging me:

"Let's go inside; it's a shootout!"

In Comuna Trece, there are people with guns. Jorge and his girlfriend were friends of Amparo. They lived two houses from hers, and her mom cried a lot. When they buried him, many people cried. Some friends fired into the air and cried. His mom fainted. Poor thing. My mom worries when I go to La Villa because she thinks a car might run over me. I think she would be very sad if she found out that I'm really going to Comuna Trece. I don't know why. They don't let Hugo go because they steal his bicycle that his mom sent him from New York. Since I don't have a bicycle from New York or Medellín, they don't steal anything from me. Besides, I'm his friend. I tell everyone:

"What's g-o-o-ing on?"

And they say...

—*"Hello Lu-do-vi-i-i-ico!"*

These days, my mom bought me a phone to carry in my pocket. Hugo calls it a cellphone. She bought it so I can call her often when I go jogging. While my brother-in-law and I talked, he promised to take me to a place where they sell Hammer cars because there are few in Medellín.

"I l-l-l-love y-y-y-yellow h-h-h-hammer ca-arr!" — I told him.

He promised to take a photo of me sitting in a Hammer and was sure he could get me their catalogs. By the time we arrived at the airport, we had talked about many things.

Artur arrived. I liked seeing him with his big belly. He looked like a lady about to have babies. He was fat. What a bother, that Artur so fat. I liked his boots. They are the same as the ones in the gun movies where men shoot while riding horses and kill Indians with feathers on their heads. Artur looks like one of the men in those movies. He always wears blue pants, black boots, and shirts with stripes or big checks, but he doesn't have a hat or a horse. Instead, he drives a big black truck. A truck with big tires that he climbs onto like climbing a horse. It's very funny. I love him a lot because he makes us laugh. I never understand his jokes, but I always laugh because he only tells jokes. That Artur is really good. I love him a lot. He arrived dragging a small suitcase with wheels. I thought he would bring one like mine. When he saw us, he seemed happy, I thought. I was happy too, and I was sure of that. He hugged me first and then Tomás. I felt embarrassed with my brother-in-law because he should have hugged him first. Then I thought that my brother-in-law is a good person and doesn't get angry about things like that.

Artur greeted me like everyone else at home or outside:

—*"Hello Lu-do-vi-i-i-ico!"*

"Wha-a-at's up?" — I replied as I always do when they greet me like that.

Then he said:

"How skinny you are!"

Right from the start, I didn't understand why he used those words, and I hadn't seen him in many years. As always, I leaned in closer to him, urging him to repeat himself. He said again, pinching my belly, loud and slow for me to comprehend:

"You're... very skinny!"

I felt happy because I don't like being fat, honestly. Being fat like my mom is a hassle. In contrast, Irina and my dad are thin like me. Equally good looking like me. I took the opportunity to reply:

"Y-y-yo-u v-v-very f-f-fat, Irina and d-dad... s-skinny. B-b-beautiful."

And I laughed at him. He did too, patting his belly and making me envious because my belly wasn't as big as his.

Finally, we reached the end of the airport. Artur told my brother-in-law that he had a very nice Cherokee, and the engine sounded good. He liked hearing that. I still thought he should buy a new car and throw this one in the trash. I told them:

"Th-th-th-this car is v-v-v-very o-o-old, throw it in th-th-th-the tr-trash!"

But they didn't hear me; they were busy talking. Artur asked my brother-in-law about my parents, and he said they were fine, although my mom was delicate. I didn't know what delicate meant, but I thought it must be something good because she was with us and I had seen her laugh at Eleonora's house. He told him about my dad, saying he seemed okay but deafer than before. I didn't know what deaf meant either. I would ask Eleonora or my brother-in-law when I saw him alone and remembered to ask. I thought, though, being deaf isn't bad because he's still with us, even if he laughs less than my mom.

When we arrived home, they opened the door, and everyone settled in. One after the other because there were many of us, and not everyone could fit in the front. They let my mom and dad out first. I think they knew we had arrived by the sound of the car's engine, or maybe they saw us arrive through the window. I say this because they came out before we even got out of the car or touched the door. Similar to when I hear Igor's car noise when he comes to eat lunch at our house in Medellín.

"Hello, Arturitooooo!"

Eleonora greeted enthusiastically, waving her hand, while my mom and dad smiled happily. Artur got out of the car and ran to hug them, starting with my dad. It had been a few years since he had them close. This time, Eleonora was the last to receive a hug. I thought I was always the last when it came to hugs. It made me laugh. Eleonora was hugged last. Artur picked up the kids like a good dad. He's Patty's dad, my niece, just like my nephews Eduardito and Camila, but much older. She's twenty now and works in Chicago. Too bad she didn't come with Artur. I remember her when she was little, like Camila. But I couldn't say how she is now. I think she looks a lot like Artur because in the family, people resemble each other. Like how I look like Boris or Fausto, and they look like my dad or mom. But it's strange: neither Irina, nor Eleonora, nor Raisa look like my mom.

Now there were eight of us at Eleonora's house. Too many to fit in the Cherokee, too many to sleep in that small house. And to think we would be sixteen by the end of the week.

Artur told them things that made everyone burst into laughter. Artur always tells them things that make them laugh. From what I can imagine, he tells them about himself, his dogs, his house, his boat, his friends, and his daughter. I think most of what he tells them has to do with his daughter. I imagine this because people with children always want to talk about them. I say this also because my mom always talks about me when she entertains guests. I would also like to have children to always talk about them, but since I don't, I prefer to talk about my siblings or my parents, my most similar children. I think Artur also told them things I'll never understand, things I'll never find out about. And I think it was like that because sometimes they stopped laughing and became very serious. They became serious, and sometimes they looked at me discreetly, one by one. They looked at me, and when they met my vacant gaze, they smiled as if not wanting to break away from the conversation they were having or wanting me to join them or something similar. Somehow, I also understood that what they were talking about was serious, and the last thing I wanted was to bother them. It has been so many years of watching them talk that I've become accustomed to recognizing their gestures, their looks, their movements. Apparently, they were talking about me, something very serious because they didn't laugh, and whenever they spoke, they looked at my mom, and many times they looked at my dad, old Oslo, who kept squeezing his eyes repeatedly, hurried, and salivating his lips eagerly, making a kissing sound. Eleonora occasionally approached him and patted his shoulder to calm him down. Then Artur came up with another nonsense and pulled them out of the concern they seemed to have, and they burst into another big laughter and continued laughing and laughing.

After talking for a couple of hours, they decided to go explore Miami and see the sea. It would be great to see the sea of Miami again. The sea in Miami is very beautiful. It's beautiful, although I prefer the sea in Puerto Aventuras. In Puerto Aventuras, you can see colorful fish in the water even if you don't have your eyes submerged. I mean, you can see the fish from the outside. I'll ask my brother-in-law when he'll take us back to Puerto Aventuras. I'll ask him to get me one of those big glasses, green or blue, to see the fish inside the sea without my eyes hurting. I had never seen so many colorful fish together as when we were in Puerto Aventuras. I remember going with Irina too. She had a yellow swimsuit she wore when we went to the sea. But... well, Miami's sea is beautiful too, despite the absence of colorful fish on the shore, it's beautiful. Not like New York's sea, Anatoli's sea, which is black, deep like the sadness I sometimes feel when I see the days arriving on the terrace of my house in Medellín, the nights arriving, the days passing, and the nights too.

We had a bit of trouble before leaving the house because we wanted to use the bathroom before getting into the car. That was a problem. A time problem because we had to wait a long time to get out. Truthfully, only the men had to wait, and I had gotten used to it. Especially because my mom takes a long time before leaving. Every time I have to wait for her, I look at the watch Fausto gave me for Christmas, and I notice that it takes up to thirty other ticks for her to come out with her purse hanging from her shoulder and smelling of the latest perfume someone sent her from... London, Key West, Miami, New York, or Bradenton. It's always like that. She bathes in perfume. She puts so much on that I have to sneeze and scratch my palate with my tongue. How desperate I feel when that happens. Sometimes I get really upset, really angry. I try not to say anything, but since I can't control my sneezes, I have to tell her:

"Yy-yy-yyou, tt-ttoo mmuch pp-perfume, Mm-mom, I vvvery ss-sick, hh-how aa-an-nyo-o-oing pp-perfume!"

She tells me that soon, the perfume will stop smelling. That I endure it a bit while the perfume fades away. That I cover my nose. In other words, not to bother her, because... supposedly, just as the sneeze came, it will go away. One thing she always tells me is that she can never stop using her perfumes. I know she puts them on because she doesn't like being without a scent when she meets other ladies at the supermarket, whether she knows them or not.

She's always right: the sneeze goes away on its own, just as it appeared. The smell of perfume is very similar to the smell of being happy or not being happy, or being scared or not being scared, or being awake or not being awake. I think everything one feels that cannot be touched is like the smell of perfumes that come and soon leave, or that are there and then not. They arrive many times without one having called them. But something that always happens is that, just like being happy, scared, or something similar, the perfumes never stay... unless one pours a whole bottle on themselves. A perfume out of its bottle is like the smell of being content. When I feel that I'm not content, because I can't see Amparo, I feel like a bottle of perfume that hasn't been opened. Not being content is like that for me, and Amparo's smile is like the perfume that comes out when the bottle is opened and makes me sneeze with happiness .

Now I think that being content is always there, hidden in bottles covered with many colors, big or small, round, elongated, with red, black, green, blue caps, or even with the color of Camila's dolls' clothes. And only when there's a reason, they come out and enter everyone's noses because one's contentment can be felt by others. When I see a smile from Amparo, in my thoughts, I see that there's a reason to be content.

Then, a little bit of contentment comes out of my bottle and I spread it all over my body. Sometimes, I spread a lot, just like my mom does when she goes to the supermarket. I spread it so much that others feel that I'm filled with happiness, so... it's others who have to sneeze.

Finally, my mom came out of the bathroom, and my sisters went in. They entered but didn't take as long. They didn't take long because they already knew that both my dad and Artur and I had fierce looks from waiting in the car, dying to pee. We would pee somewhere outside the house, once we finally got out. We peed at a Burger King a few minutes later.

We went out to explore the streets of Miami. Squeezed into my brother-in-law's car, but happy. Artur drove the Cherokee. He drove it because my brother-in-law thought he should since he was the fattest. That made me understand with a very funny gesture that made me laugh —*Ar-tur is so-o-o fat... wha-a-a-t a ha-a-a-ssle, so-o-o fat, Ar-tur.*—. My mommy accompanied him in the front because she was the fattest too. My brother-in-law himself invited her to sit in the front, opening the car door for her and helping her get in. She got in as if mounting a horse because the car was rather high for her. What a pity that my mom, being so old, gets into a car like mounting a horse. I understood that too because my brother-in-law made me understand it again, with another gesture he pretended not to make obvious so that my mom wouldn't notice. The smell of perfume made all of us sneeze, but no one dared to want to inconvenience my mom. I, for my part, couldn't stand it and said grumbling:

"Hoow bo-bo-bother-s-ome, moo-om, y-oou wi-wi- with soo mu-uch perfu-ume, me, ve-very siick, whaat a bo- bo-bother, perfu-u-me!"

And she replied for everyone to hear: "I'm very sorry, my dear!"

I understood why she always replied the same, and she was right. The sneeze went away, not just mine, but everyone's, including little Eduardito's. Irina, Eleonora, and Camila didn't sneeze. I think because they are women, and women are the ones who wear more perfume when they go out, so they are used to it.

We arrived at a place near the sea. A large restaurant with many tables and boats outside, moored, like the horses in the movies whose owners look like Artur. Everyone was talking to each other. So, I took the opportunity to look at the sea and those big birds with bags in their beaks. My brother-in-law told me they are called pelicans. Everyone in my family was talking and laughing at times; other times, laughing and talking, until Eleonora had the idea to go out and dance with little Camila in her arms. I think to make her fall asleep because she was being cranky and didn't let them talk. Now, not only were they talking and laughing, but they were also dancing. Since I didn't talk or dance, I just laughed when I saw gestures that piqued my curiosity or seemed funny to me.

Later, Eleonora asked me, making gestures with her face and hands: "Ludovico, are you hungry?"

It was good that she asked because I was indeed hungry. However, the smell of the sea made me feel that fishy smell I have always detested. That's when I replied:

"*I-I-I do-o-o-on't li-i-i-ike f-f-f-fish.*"

"Then... would you like steak with French fries?" she asked.

"*Yee-ss, Yee-ss, Ye-e-s-s.*"

She ordered steak for me with lots of French fries. I love French fries! I waited for the food while I asked my brother-in-law about the other birds, different from the pelicans, and the boats still moored like horses.

We played which boat we liked the most. I asked my mom which one she liked, so I could agree with her. She always helps me choose things when I have to pick, and even though she doesn't know much about boats because there are none in Medellín, she helped me. It was very fun. I chose a different boat than the one my mom recommended. I preferred a not-so-big one because inside it, I could see a beautiful woman, with yellow hair and a pretty face. A woman just like the ones in the movies I watch at night before going to sleep. A woman like those who make me stretch my tutu and make me tremble and tremble with happiness... One of those. Yes, she was one of those... I was so captivated because when she turned her body to step into the shade of the boat, it left my eyes astonished. Her round buttocks were so beautiful that I wouldn't even have liked the string of her green swimsuit to touch them. In Medellín, there are no women with yellow hair, but there are many with buttocks as beautiful as hers. In Medellín, almost all the pretty women have black or brown hair. I like boats where there are very beautiful women like Amparo. She is very beautiful. I miss Amparo when I remember her.

There was music in that place, played by a man with green eyes, dark skin, and long messy hair, as if he had bits of dirt hanging from it, and he played the piano while singing. He sang very nicely. I like people who, when they sing nicely, play the piano... It makes one feel happy. Those people are like the perfume that escapes from its bottle, and its smell reaches everyone, making us sneeze with happiness. He was a different man, very unlike most men. His hair looked more like strips of hanging cloth, but, anyway, it was his real hair. I'm sure of that because I looked at it almost all the time. He sang beautifully. His music was very cheerful. So cheerful that a lady, also dark-skinned, danced. She was a very beautiful lady; she looked like his wife because she smiled at him, and he smiled back at her. She was as beautiful as she could be, with big buttocks and small breasts. I say small because they didn't come out of a small red bra that covered them from the front. The other people were also dancing. I'm not embarrassed to dance, but I don't like to do it. I think it's because people stare at me a lot. My eyes just don't stay still when I look. Sometimes they move so much that I can't even see what I need to see. When that happens, when my eyes move very quickly, I go to my mom and tell her that my eyes are naughty. She tells me to sit next to her for a while, and if my eyes don't stay still, to let her know so she can give me half a pill. But when she gives me that half pill, I don't feel like dancing or laughing anymore. I feel like crying and not being content, and I stop being quick. That's when I move away from everyone and don't feel like laughing when everyone else does. When my mom gives me half a pill, I feel like the sea in New York, still, without colorful fishes. Not like the sea in Puerto Aventuras, which has them and can be seen from the outside. I sat close to my mother, thinking that I should be alone, still, standing, like when I stand in front of Eleonora's window, watching birds like when I'm in Medellín, or watching lizards like when I'm in Miami. I only know how to watch people dance by moving my eyes almost always. Sometimes my eyes don't move restlessly and I see better. Eleonora asked me to dance, but I didn't feel like it. I preferred to stay trying to guess what my mom, my dad, and Artur were talking about. Once again, I stayed there, concentrated on trying to understand them, but dumb and withdrawn in front of their eyes. It was difficult for me to know what they were talking about. It was impossible. I remember they said something like they didn't know what to do with an old piece of furniture my mom has in the house in Medellín. I remember my mom said:

"That's why we made this long trip."

I thought they were talking about the piece of furniture where my mom keeps glass items that she receives as gifts during Christmas or that Fausto sends her. Fausto is the one who sends her the most glass items. My mom calls them "crystal." Every time she asks me to bring her a crystal to put her flowers in, I find myself thinking... Could it be that crystal is also called glass? Because what I see is that my mom's crystals are made of glass, just like the ones in the windows of my house. It's just that Fausto loves my mom a lot. I think he loves her the most out of all of us because he also sends her smaller things where she keeps her rings, earrings, and other things that make her happy. My mom keeps some U.S. dollars in a wooden box inside the wardrobe where the big, brown-skinned woman irons the clothes every Friday. My dad never knows where my mom keeps the bills tied up in a big roll that everyone gives her. Especially Fausto and Anatoli, the one from New York. My dad also has money, but it's in the bank. I think my dad has a lot of money because whenever my mom goes to the supermarket, she pays with my dad's money. My siblings never give money to my dad. When my dad runs out of pocket money, he goes to the bank and gets more. All dads get money from the bank. I am sure that I love my mom more than Fausto because I accompany her to the supermarket every day, no matter that her perfume makes me sneeze. When someone comes home to greet my mom, my dad, and me, my mom takes out the plates from that piece of furniture they were talking about with Artur. I remember my mom asked Artur:

"Would you take care of him?"

"Difficult. I am not yet an American citizen, and

I wouldn't know how to bring it to Chicago—" Artur replied.

I knew what he said, but I didn't understand him. I didn't even understand what he meant. That always happens. What does a citizen have to do with that piece of furniture? Later, Artur said something like…

"Besides, I have problems because I drove drunk, and they might deport me to Colombia."

I did understand that because "drunk" means the same here and in Medellín. I know a lot about drunks. I've been around them for forty-four years. What a laugh. They've lived with me my entire life. I also know drunks who aren't around anymore because they got run over by a car while being drunk. Like Don Chepe, Mrs. Elvira's husband, who got run over by a bus in Don Quixote's roundabout. A drunk is someone who likes to stop being what they are every day, like when they wake up after sleeping and prefer to be something people shouldn't be. I think being drunk is nice when you're not too drunk, when you're just starting to get drunk. I mean when you've only had a couple of beers and not as quickly as Fausto drinks them, because he really gets drunk then and stops being himself. He starts laughing at everything that isn't funny, starts bothering those who are calm, and his mouth starts smelling like a dog's mouth, and his eyes squint, and he starts acting like a fool. He wants to drink more and more, wants to dance even with a broom or a janitor, and he doesn't want to go to bed when everyone else wants to sleep. He doesn't want to go inside the house and leaves the door open, and because he's drunk, he doesn't realize that mosquitoes are getting inside, biting all of us. So I have to get up to scratch my arms, legs, face, and I have to ask my mom to kill that damn mosquito that's bothering me at night. My mom gets up with a towel pretending to kill it, but being old, she can't do it because the damn mosquito hides. So, I have to sleep covered up to my head so that the damn mosquito doesn't bother me that much. And the next day, I wake up all messed up because of it, and Fausto doesn't care at all because he never even notices that his drunkenness ends up making me do that nonsense I do sometimes. A lot of things happen because of a drunk who drinks two beers too quickly or many beers in the end.

The truth is that Artur told my mom that he couldn't bring an old piece of furniture because he had driven drunk, and something else… and they stayed silent for a while, sad, looking at each other and looking at me from time to time, discreetly. I suppose they became sad instead… I thought Artur didn't get drunk anymore in Chicago, that he had stopped getting drunk when he left Colombia, but apparently people get drunk here too. How annoying drunks are. Anyway, I didn't understand what they talked about, although I paid attention. I dared to ask Artur, trying to help him get out of that sadness:

"Wh-when did y-you see M-mom's o-old fu-furniture in C-Co-Colombia, wh-when?"

Artur explained to me that he wouldn't travel to

Colombia because he had a lot of work in Chicago. So I said what I always say when something I didn't want to happen happens:

"Hoow ba-aa-dd. Don't ddrink m-more be-er, ve-ery druunk?"

Artur smiled, but not very happily. It seemed that what I said caught his attention, but not enough to laugh like everyone laughs at his jokes. Apparently, mine wasn't a real joke or was a bad joke. Artur spoke again after being silent for a while, while they looked at each other, and he looked at people dancing as if to distract himself or not look at the old people or at me. He said something like...

"Calm down, mom. If something happens to you, I'll go back to Colombia, and I'll take care of him."

He also said...

"It doesn't matter if I can't come back to Chicago." And again, he fell silent. Then he finished saying:

"Stay calm, old lady."

And he approached her, hugged her, and kissed her on the forehead. That seemed strange to me because Artur is funny, but I had never seen him hugging my mom, let alone giving her kisses with sorrow. My mom looked at me, and her eyes gleamed as if she wanted to cry. As if she were talking about me or wanted to tell me something with her wet eyes. I felt sad for her, wanted to reassure her:

"Tha-aat o-oo-old fu-uu-r-nitu-ure, to-oo the-e-e-e traa-ash!"

My brother-in-law, who was just listening, spoke

as well:

"Calm down, Mrs. Anastasia. It's very difficult for Artur to take care of it. Let's wait for everyone to arrive, and we'll decide what to do."

Again, I was confused by many words that I couldn't understand, but that told me some suffering of my mom. She, however, didn't want to accept throwing her old furniture away, and they stayed silent again. I don't like seeing my mom sad because of an old piece of furniture. I think to avoid seeing her like that, I got up from the table and walked to the front of the boat where the woman with yellow hair was. I watched her while thinking about Amparo. When the woman noticed that I was watching her, she smiled, but at the same time, she hid. Surely, she felt afraid or wanted to go to the bathroom to pee. How good it was that I thought about Amparo because my sadness about seeing my mom sad disappeared. I know when my mom is sad. I know because she gets angry about everything. In contrast, my dad never gets angry, well, almost never, or better once a day. He usually stays silent on the third floor filling out the newspaper crosswords and listening to the music sent by my brother-in-law so as not to be near my mom when she's sad or angry for being sad.

My dad always listens to music without singers. Music with only pianos or guitars, but I like reggaeton. The music my dad listens to is for old people like him, who are eighty and more.

We left the place in a hurry to greet Irina. She's everyone's favorite in the family. I know because when

I was very little, some men entered our house and beat us up to steal a sound system that arrived from the United States sent by Anatoli. Irina suffered a lot because they kicked her in the face, leaving her in bad shape. How good that she's okay now and sends me Christmas or birthday gifts. Eleonora also sends me gifts from Miami. Especially video games. The last one they sent me was a very good car racing game. I'm very good at car racing games. I almost always beat Hugo. It's because Hugo is slow with his fingers and his gaze, and I'm very fast with my fingers, although with my gaze, sometimes slower than him.

70

With Nonsense and All

Irina finally arrived, I thought to myself, and just as I expected, she greeted me first, waving her right hand even while she was still inside the car.

She arrived in the new Volkswagen, a color I was eager to see. I liked seeing Irina in her soft gray clothes, her slender body as always. She never wears dresses that don't have long pants, never. All my life, I've seen her in long pants. I don't recall ever seeing her in skirts or dresses where her legs could be seen. I know she has beautiful legs because I saw them one day at the beach when they took us to Puerto Aventuras. She thinks her legs are ugly, maybe they are, although she's never told me. Perhaps she doesn't believe in them enough to show them off like ugly and pretty women do? I remember she hurried into the sea, trying to cover her body with water. When she came out, she quickly ran to hide it, wearing a long robe she had brought and left on the sand, ready to put on when she emerged.

She's a solitary person. She always has been, growing up and even now. She got used to it, I would say. She's as lonely as I tend to be. Even now, as she's grown almost old, she remains solitary, perhaps more than me, because I leave my house to greet friends who know me, but she doesn't. She never leaves her house because she's afraid of people, because she thinks people will embarrass her or who knows what. I think she came to visit us today because it's about us, her parents and me, and because we hadn't seen each other for many years.

Irina lives alone, apart from everyone and everything. She only looks for my father on Wednesdays, by phone, when she calls to subtly convey her love for him and show she's keeping an eye on him. She calls him to help find a word my old man can't locate to complete his crossword puzzles. That's when she lets me talk on the phone, and she greets me. Wednesday is Irina's day to call Colombia; she never misses it. She always calls at eight in the evening. I know it's her when the phone rings that day, at that hour, and I'm home to hear it ring.

When my old lady hears the phone ring, she pretends not to hear it because she's watching her soap opera on TV. But the phone rings and rings, so she yells, "Oslo, answer the phone; it must be Irina with the crossword."

Then, my old man doesn't answer because he's distracted or already asleep, or pretending to watch television, and my mother has to stop watching her soap opera and answer the phone. It's almost always Irina. So, my mother, to not miss her soap opera, answers hurriedly:

"Hello... hello, dear, how are you? I'll pass you to

your dad; I'm watching my soap opera."

Then, she yells again, and my dad finally realizes it's for him. When my mother feels my dad pick up the phone and says, "hello, dear," and Irina replies, "hello, dad," she hangs up and goes back to watching her eight o'clock soap opera. Irina loves my old man very much. I know this from her dedication. She never wants my old man to be alone, that's why she calls him on Wednesdays. Sometimes, when the old folks are a bit sick and need to go to the doctor often, she travels to Medellín and takes care of them. Before going back to Bradenton, she leaves me a note with the days and times when they need to take the pills the doctor prescribed, and I help take care of them that way. When she returns to the United States, I remind them of the times they should take their pills and even bring them a glass of milk or water for them to take them. I like helping the elderly take their pills. I like it.

Has Irina accustomed herself since she was a little girl to living in fear or dread...? How I wish to think it's not so. From what I see, she always maintains that desire not to be seen or noticed. I don't feel the same because when someone comes to the house, I go out so everyone can see me. What does it matter if they see me like this, with my disobedient or stubborn eyes and my ears that are deaf or mute? I don't care if people who come to my house are frightened by me—if they don't know me—or if they wonder what I meant if I said something and they didn't understand, or because they talk to me and I don't understand them, or if they have to ask my old lady what I said, or if they have to ask my old lady to tell them something that they are not capable of telling me, or if, having tried to tell me, I haven't heard them, or if, having heard them, I haven't understood them... What do I care about all of that, if I'm not embarrassed, I have never been embarrassed. My old lady taught me that shame should never appear in my head. That I should never hide, even if people laugh at me. One thing I do know about Irina is that everyone likes her, and I don't understand why she's so lonely. On the other hand, people in my house or those who get to know me after realizing that I'm not crazy and that I like being a good friend, that I enjoy being close to them no matter that I can't talk to them often, are the only ones who like me. With Irina, everyone would like to be laughing, talking, walking, but she prefers to be alone always, it doesn't matter that she's pretty, it doesn't matter that, although being pretty, she's now older and lonelier, distant from everyone, distant in a nice house where you can't hear the music, where you can't see the television, in a small city that, though clean, has no people in its streets, where there is no one to visit her and to whom she can say:

"He-e- e-llooo, guu-uys! Ho-o-ow a-re y-y-ou?" And they would answer her... *"He-e-e-llooo, I-i-rina, o-o-ow be-a-a-utiful y-y-ou are!"*

She lives in a very nice house, one of those houses that gets photographed in magazines, with a living room from where you can see people playing golf next to a lake where fish jump happily or want to eat a fly that passed by. There lives Irina, only accompanied by ants that suddenly find themselves eating crumbs of bread she can't clean up because they are very small and she can't see them. Those little pieces that only ants can see. When someone asks about Irina, they do it with joy, I've noticed that. Everyone asks about Irina with affection, as if they knew something about her that makes them sad. It's something I can't comprehend. The truth is that people ask about her eagerly, but she's almost never there, so it's pointless to ask. It makes me laugh when someone comes to the house and I go out, then the newcomer gets scared if they don't know me yet. If I were Irina, I would walk around my body and show my legs so that all those who wanted to see them would see them, so that, when they saw them, they would think things like what I think when I see the bodies of girls, like when I see Amparo's body with or without clothes, with or without smiles, with or without dreams. It's very cute. Now that I remember it, when I was little, a man with a white beard liked her very much, old I would say, very old for her when she was young and went to school.

He was an old man who wanted to be her friend every day, every night, and who suddenly wanted to have children with her, why not? He pursued her, reached the corner of the house, and signaled for her to come out, but my mom wouldn't let her out. And as she wanted to see him, my mom punished her, punished her so she wouldn't go out, and locked her up and scolded her. That went on for many years, during those years when Irina was the prettiest in the neighborhood, the prettiest in Laureles, but also the saddest. I think Irina got tired of being liked by that man when she was just a young girl. Young like Amparo. I think she got tired of waiting for him to see her so they could talk like people who like each other do, and they talk and hold hands and touch their bodies each and they give kisses to each other, and when they're alone, they lie down because they're embarrassed that people might see them, like in the movies I watch at night before sleeping. But that never happened with them because my mother was very angry, so angry that she punished all of us if we saw that man nearby and didn't tell her. She punished us very harshly, more my brothers than me because she never punished me, but she did punish them. Because they came home late, because they didn't clean the house, because they didn't do their chores, and for other reasons I wouldn't be able to explain. Is that why Irina ended up alone? Is she still waiting for that man to come to the corner and call her? Does she still want to go to him and kiss him, hug him, and touch him? What a pity for Irina. She stayed alone waiting for the man with the white beard who never returned because my mother kept it from her. Let's say Irina is the only one of my three sisters who grew old without having a boyfriend, or friends who stayed overnight with her. I will never understand why she's alone, watching people play golf from a distance, waiting for others to leave so she can take her turn, hoping that silence will accompany her and not music.

The truth is Irina arrived in her Volkswagen. She usually greets me first every time she has to choose whom to greet first when she sees the three of us. It seems like she loves me more than Eleonora, although I don't think so. Eleonora is more serious when it comes to showing affection. That is to say, less embarrassing, more determined, more... cool. Eleonora is my friend when I need to tell her about the late-night television I watch, and to whom I share some things about Amparo and the people from the neighborhoods. And she enjoys me telling her, it's obvious, she doesn't feel embarrassed with me. That night, they all talked a lot until it was time to go to bed. I remember Irina brought an inflatable mattress in the trunk of her car, with a device that plugs into the wall to inflate it. That night, I slept on that mattress, as we were already nine. It was simple and fun. My mom and dad must have slept in Eleonora's bed, Irina in little Eduardito's bed next to Camila, Eduardito and Artur on the square sofa in front of the largest TV, and I on the inflatable mattress.

It wasn't hard to do it. The hard part was sleeping despite Artur's snoring, which sounds louder when he lies down drunk. I've known it since he was in the house and he would go to bed drunk. That night, he almost drank a bottle of aguardiente, accompanied by Eleonora, who occasionally had one with lemon juice. We went to bed at two in the morning, but soon someone knocked on the door, scaring us. It seemed like Eleonora was expecting someone because she jumped up like a spring. When that someone knocked on the door, I got scared because I wasn't completely asleep and because I was thinking instead of sleeping. Artur didn't even notice; he kept snoring. I was afraid that someone would knock at these hours, and I ran to Eleonora and told her I was scared.

"Wow, wha-a-a-t a sc-ca-a-are!"

"Don't be scared, it's Boris. Lie down!" —she responded.

Noticing my puzzled expression, she repeated it softly twice until I understood. 'She asked me to go back to sleep,' I thought, wrapping myself up and leaving my face uncovered to look. It had been months since I last saw Boris. I noticed he was fat, much fatter than in Medellín. The smell of alcohol was identical to when he said goodbye because he was coming to Miami. Eleonora kissed him on the cheek and hugged him. Noticing everything in the dark, swaying, Boris tried to go back to the street. She took him by the hand and invited him to stay. Then she closed the door. I noticed she said something to him and then led him to the kitchen. I decided to sleep, thinking about Amparo. I imagined her smiling, as she always does when she's happy, and although I wanted to see her face on the bodies of the women in the early morning movies, I didn't. Suddenly, I felt ashamed of wetting my pajamas, and it would be Eleonora who would wash the clothes, not my mom. I talked for a while with Amparo; I remember we talked about old furniture. In a piece of furniture in her living room, she keeps many U.S. dollars that her friends bring to buy new Hammer or Cherokee.

The next day, at some point, I woke up to Boris's curses and everyone's laughter. Surely Artur said something that made them laugh. The noise, the obscenities, the laughter didn't bother me. I woke up calm, without anger for not being able to talk to everyone or anyone, or not being able to share things like they do when people gather to talk. I just wanted to greet them and imagine how each of those missing might be to decide what to do with my mom's old furniture. Anyway, he's my brother, I thought, regardless of whether he's drunk or says words like... son of a bitch, what an asshole, or that damn fool. My dad doesn't like Boris because he's a drunk and because he fights a lot with my mom because of him.

My dad fainted when he was taking a shower, in April, and Boris was the one who took him to the hospital. That day, my mom and I were at the supermarket buying the usual with the money my dad leaves on the dining table before going up to do the Sunday crosswords. It's weird that when my dad was in the hospital, I didn't cry like I did with my mom. I think men are less necessary than women. That's what I think, because of my mom and because of Eleonora. I'd rather Tomás die first than Eleonora because she's the one who helps Eduardito and Camila have clean clothes. Besides, she cooks the tastier food. That's strange because on TV, men are the ones who make the tastiest food, always the men wearing white caps. I've thought that women cook at home and men in restaurants. My brother-in-law has never cooked, only when we go to the beach and have a barbecue. The day my dad got sick, when my mom and I went to the supermarket, the taxi driver who took us sneezed because of my mom's perfume. I knew he had sneezed because of the perfume, and my mom knew it too. However, I didn't say anything, and neither did my mom. Surely, if the taxi driver had known he sneezed because of the old lady's perfume, he would have charged us more for the ride. Taxi drivers probably never imagine why they sneeze every time ladies full of perfume get in.

Boris has been living in Miami since my dad left the hospital. I think he came to avoid being home when my dad returned. I found out by overhearing my mom saying something similar on the phone with Amparo, León's wife. Many times, Boris had to leave the house when my dad got furious with my mom and yelled at her, "I don't understand how such an old man spends all day in this house saying obscenities and drinking aguardiente." Sometimes my mom replies, "I told you not to go drinking with him when he was young."

That makes me laugh because my dad gets angrier, but he doesn't say anything more and stays silent or walks away, or acts like it's not about him. Maybe that's why the old man rarely says things my mom doesn't like, like talking badly about Boris.

The next four days passed quickly. They talked a lot, smiled; we even went to the beach and did other things only done in Miami. We enjoyed being all together, although on the fifth day, I woke up with the nonsense in my head and doing things I shouldn't, like every time it happens to me. I shouted at my mom with bad words I learned as a child listening to Artur, Boris, Igor, and Anatoli. I learned them from hearing people in the neighborhood, from the block, when something pleases them or displeases them, when they're angry and happy. They've never said them to offend us; they just say them because they didn't learn to talk without saying them. I can read their lips and understand when they say them smiling, calmly, or furiously. I think they like saying them as much as they like smoking cigarettes, drinking beer or aguardiente, or smoking marijuana like my sister, the one in London, and her husband Randy. What I don't understand is that throughout my life, I've only used those words to shout at my dear old mom, every time I wake up with the nonsense. Fausto doesn't say them, only when he's a little drunk... something like Artur, but not as much as Boris. I think it was very hard for everyone to see my outbursts of madness. It's just that when I'm like this, everyone who has given me happiness turns into strange things with faces of people I know or have seen sometime when I was little or grown-up. Things that have no legs, no arms, no mouth, and move like pale-colored fish with sharp teeth, with wrinkles on their foreheads like they're suffering, with sad looks, so sad that it makes me want to cry. It's just that when I get this nonsense, I see people's faces on bodies of elephants running and running towards me to crush me, and I run and run, but they catch up with me and step on me while shouting frantically. When I get like this, people from the street come to my house to throw stones at the windows and wooden and iron doors, and I hear the windows when the glass breaks. I feel people shouting at me to run out, naked, and they laugh at me and their stones hit me on the back, on the head, on the legs... I feel many green mosquitoes biting my face, and I shoo them away, but they don't leave. Then, I have to scratch my face, my back, my arms, my legs, and I even draw blood from scratching. I feel, feel, and feel until my mother gives me the pill so I don't feel it anymore. How sad for my mom when I get like this. Her face isn't serene like always. But how can it be serene if with the nonsense, I tell her, right to her face, clenching my teeth and my hands:

"Yo-u bit-ch. Not me. Bi-t-ch! Bit-c-h! And I'm fu-u-rioo-us!"

And I make her blink because of the saliva I spit out with the obscenities that come out of my mouth. I can't help it, although I really wanted to on this trip. Something like what happens to the dog when she poops in the living room because she can't go out to the yard. I saw them nervous, pretending they didn't see me or hear me. I needed one of them to punch me in the face to make me sleep like in the movies, but none of them dared. My mom had forbidden them from doing that. Fausto was the most concerned of the men because the women didn't know where to go. The only one standing and brave, holding onto my thread of life, was my mom. The kids cried terrified because of my tantrums, and my brother-in-law took them to the front yard. I was out of control for hours, two or three, until my mother finally convinced me to take the pill. I think this has been one of the longest agonies of my life. When I thought I was gaining control, I would return to my mom's face and shout at her again:

"You bit-ch!"

I repeated it knowing that my only desire was to await his scolding to figure out what to do. The devil entered inside me to make me feel bad. I saw him with horns, red eyes, dog-like teeth, and an arrow tail like the ones in movies where the good guys kill the Indians, similar to Artur. That day, I turned into a devil for having forgotten something in Medellín and feeling that no one would understand me when I tried to explain it. Whenever I want to talk about something, I need to give examples or demonstrate it. When I want cold water, I have to make my mom understand that I'm sweating, running my fingers over my forehead and saying:

"So hot..."

But when I want cold water and I'm not sweating, then she doesn't understand, and I have to serve the water myself. Now I serve water when I have and don't have sweat. My mom must have thought I was angry about something similar. I've been getting angry about silly things for forty-four years. That day my mom remained silent out of shame with everyone. Especially with my brother-in-law and the kids for being new in front of me and not as old as all my brothers put together.

The day I drew my mom how I see my body when I'm angry, she told me that only by going to mass with Priest Pio would my anger go away. She has always told me that Priest Pio is like a policeman who protects me from the devil. I felt like going to him, and with determination, I said, *"Me-e-e-e and you-u-u to mas-s-s-s. pri-iest Pio-o-o."*

And I walked away to the garden where my brother-in-law was playing with my nephews to distract them. He greeted me with a big smile, but with sorrow. Both he and I knew that I was going through a bad time. However, he didn't hint at any discomfort. The little ones seemed afraid of seeing me and eagerly sought my brother-in-law's eyes. He asked me, walking with his fingers of his right hand on his left palm:

"Do you want to walk?"

"To-oo whe-ee-ere?"

"Over there, on the golf course."

'I would have liked to understand quickly,' I thought. He pretended to be hitting a ball on the ground with an invisible club. I remembered he had told me, two days ago, that his house, although very old and ugly, was close to a golf course. I got more excited to forget than to walk. I thought of mom and got sad. I guessed that later, when I was trying to sleep deeply, I would cry and suffer for not knowing how to apologize. I think it's not fair, and I said inside me: *"fo- r-r-rgivenes-s, fo-r-r-rgi-i-venes-s."*

"Wal-king-g-g?, yo-o-ou, Willll, Cami-lll-lla."

"Just you and me," he answered, pointing at me and then at himself.

¡Ah!...

He left the kids inside the house and came out immediately. We walked in silence for half a block until he asked me, making a turn with his arm almost over his head:

"Do you like this place?"

"It's ve-e-ry niii-ice. Wha-at's it call-lled?"

"Coral Gables."

He repeated the two words part by part until I managed to grasp the name, which I only stopped repeating when he approved by raising the thumb of his right hand.

"Cora-l-l-l Gab-l-ll-lls."

"We became happy," he said. He assured me they bought that old house to fix it and make it beautiful to share it with me every time I was in Miami, supposedly so that I could always be calm, walking out there, listening to birds and watching gardens with cheerful squirrels climbing palm trees and trees, or playing, balancing on the electricity wires and coming close to me when I'm eating something they want or just to see if they might like what I'm eating or not.

He assured me that, unlike Medellín, there I could play in the front yard without fear that some bad person would steal my sneakers, watch, or phone. I was glad to know that they have thought of me, as I would have never imagined it. It seemed to me that in some way, they wanted me to stay or at least tell them I would like to stay. When I think of my parents, things change because if I stay in Miami and leave them alone, surely they will die of sadness because they won't be able to worry about me not coming home early or being out on the street, and they will steal my watch, or they will take my phone, or they will shoot me, thinking I'm one of those who steal purses from ladies, or they cut earrings from girls, or they take wallets from those who are careless and let their wallets be taken. The bad people are also like me, only they see better than me and speak well, because the bad ones always speak well so that you don't notice how bad they are.

Anyway, I liked them to know that I like the animals in the garden because they are curious and entertain me when sometimes I need to chase away the urge not to do the stupid things that sometimes come to my mind. The only thing I don't like is that Eleonora's house is very old and smells old, and I don't like old things that smell old. I'll tell my brother-in-law to buy a new house and let me stay always and let the old people stay with me too, and if he can..., tell my mom to let me call Amparo and my mom tell Amparo to come live nearby, so I can go out and walk and walk with her and also bring people who know me so that when I'm walking on the street with Amparo and they see us, I can say to them:

— *"What's g-o-o-ing on?"* so they reply, *"Hello Lu-do-vi-i-i-ico!"*

And to look at her and imagine her kissing me

and hugging me and telling me nice things, like for example telling me she wants to see me, wants to hug me, or wants me to help her with chores, or one thing, or another, and making her feel happy.

We walked in silence at times while I thought about everything I've already said I was thinking about. Just two blocks away from the house, we were skirting a golf course that showed a yellow tower on the green horizon. According to him, it was a very important hotel where the soldiers from the movies they show on television stayed. To understand each other, I practiced several times with him how to call it, and we agreed that I would call it the *Ho-otell-l Bilg-gmo-o-o-rg-g*.

I compared the place to La Villa in Medellín. I did it when I saw an old man trotting by, just like my dad. In Medellín, old people don't trot; they only walk. Many of them don't even walk because they are not as fond of walking as the people here. They feel useless ever since they feel old. Do they get tired faster? In contrast, in Miami, I see them looking happy, both old men and women, driving big cars and wearing colors like green, red, and others as strange as the pink colors of Camila's dolls. The old people in Medellín are like my dad and my mom; they always dress in dark or semi-mourning colors. My mom says that the white and black in their clothes are called semi-mourning, and she always wears it because someone has died very recently. Judging by the color of the clothes of the old people in Miami, it seems like nobody ever dies for them. The old people in Medellín look alike because they are always at home, taking care of the dog and shooing away the pigeons so they won't poop on the railings when houses have railings. They also spend their time listening to the news to find out which people died that day and if any of the dead were someone we all knew.

Sometimes, when someone dies who appears on television and everyone knows, my mom calls me and tells me. Almost every time she tells me about a new death, I can't figure out who it is. So I usually wait until their photo appears on television. I know everyone who appears on television, and I can tell if they are good or bad. I almost always manage to know if someone is good or bad, but when I'm unsure, I ask my mom. She tells me, and then I start thinking of that person as either good or bad. Sometimes I don't remember what my mom told me about someone on television, and I have to ask her again. My mom is never wrong. Every time I see a person for the first time, I think I know if they are good or bad. When a good person dies or gets killed, I feel sad; but when a bad person is killed, I feel that now there are more good people. Maybe I should say that there are more good people, although today I was very bad with my mom and my family when I couldn't control my nonsense. I experienced what many in Medellín feel when people die. They do it because they feel something very strong inside that compels them to do it. When I am very angry, sometimes I feel like destroying even the image I see when I stand in front of the bathroom mirror on the second floor, but I think I must go to Priest Pio's mass, and the anger disappears like my mom's perfume scent. My mom has taught me to think of the mass when I'm feeling down. I think that if all the bad people in Medellín went to Priest Pio's mass, there wouldn't be familiar faces appearing dead on television. Maybe they would die when they are old, like my dad and my mom. I feel that there are more bad people than good people in Medellín. I know it. When I accompany my mom to the supermarket, we always think that anyone who approaches us is bad. Only when someone we know greets us do we think they are good. For me to believe that everyone on the street is good, they would have to greet us, and I don't think we have time for that because we have to go back home before it's too late and the bad people start coming out more often. I have learned that everyone on the street is bad except for the beautiful women like Amparo or the old ladies like my mom, or the women who are like my sisters. Now I am sure that only men are bad if they are not old like my dad. When I leave home during the day, my mom is at ease, but when she feels that I haven't returned before nightfall, she worries. Poor thing, she worries about me depending on the sunlight. I think she hates the night because she thinks it's full of bad people. I also think she hates it because it reminds her of the fatigue in her legs.

While I was thinking while walking, so was my brother-in-law, quietly, as if he were thinking about the same things I was thinking about. It was a walk filled with glances at each house, each garden, each squirrel, each bird. We thought and walked until I noticed that sweat appeared on my brother-in-law's forehead, but not on mine. I once asked Eleonora why I don't sweat like others who soak their clothes and look like they've wet their hair. She said it's because I'm as skinny as a twig. I remember she asked me if I had ever seen a twig sweat. It made me laugh. That Eleonora is very funny. Now I understand that skinny people hardly sweat.

In one of those steps, I remembered the blonde from the boat, but my head changed her to a woman just like Amparo. I saw her smiling at me, inviting me to enter the boat. I felt happy, and I felt my pants straighten. I wanted to be alone with her just like in the late-night movies. Other things happened around the boat that day, and I stopped thinking about her because I remembered my mom's old piece of furniture.

"D-do you kn-know old f-f-furniture... Sooo oooould... j-just like m-mom?"

I stammered.

"Furniture?" Tomás replied with interest.

"Yes, ju-u-st lik-ke moom. Re-e-member... Ar-gg-tur... mom... you... El-ll-le-o-noo-ra."

He understood my question. Maybe Artur wouldn't have understood it, although they talked about it the day we went to the restaurant where I saw the woman I dressed as Amparo today while walking. I remembered my mom with her moist little eyes that she wiped so I wouldn't see them like that. My brother-in-law explained to me that my mom worried about many things. He said that all old people worry about their old furniture and that my mom, being an old lady, is now worried about that piece of furniture. According to her, she has had it since the day I was born.

"This f-furni-i-i-ture is so-oo o-o-o-o-old, to the tr-tr-a-a-ash,"

I said while thinking about her again.

It would be best to throw it in the trash or give it to someone younger than my parents so they can have it for a longer time, and my mom won't feel bad about throwing it away in case she dies. Anyway, my mom won't be sad again. When I thought like that, sadness came back inside me. This time it came accompanied by a bit of fear, although the sadness was bigger than the fear. I remembered blinking because of the saliva I spit out when I shouted at her:

— *"You-u-u bii-itc-h!"*

I cried silently, and my brother-in-law knew it because he saw when my tears reached my nose, stinging me to make me scratch, but he didn't say anything. Not even when I wiped my hands on my pants several times. It's better not to say anything to me when I'm sad, either for myself or for my old lady or my old folks.

"I d-don't like m-my mom s-sad,"

I added.

He didn't answer. He remained silent. He approached me and grabbed my shoulder tightly. That helped me feel better. Every time I think that my old lady is very old and that she might stop being awake like what happens to those on the television news, I see myself walking alone like I am now with my brother-in-law, but in places as different as Comuna Trece in Medellín, without people who greet me or with many people who don't greet me and whom I need to say:

"Hi, Lu-do-vi-i-i-ico!" to, so they'll reply:

"Hey, ma-an."

About Things
That Resemble Others

"Is it a m-a-an or a wo-o-man?"

I asked many times that day, overheated, while we were watching zebras, elephants, tigers..., at the Miami Zoo.

When my mom doesn't know if the animal I'm asking about is a man or a woman, she asks anyone nearby, and finally, she tells me. My mom doesn't know anymore if some animals are men or women, and even less my dad, who seems more subdued than her. I don't think I'll ask my mom again. That day, taking advantage of being together on that family outing, I noticed someone different to ask. I noticed Raisa, my sister from London, who curiously was walking near me. Strange, she almost never walks close to me when she's in Medellín or when we go to London to visit her and walk around where the big clock in the photos or on television is. Raisa is the one who, when she passes through Medellín, throws those parties full of friends, aguardiente, and cigarette smoke they roll in a little white paper and fill with dry leaves. I remember that once, when Artur was still living in my house before my mom called the soldiers to take him away to run and walk with a rifle on his shoulder, he planted some plants in my backyard. He planted them, and they grew like the plants that grow in gardens or in fields, meaning they grew a little tall. I remember, when I was still very little, he would cut them and hang them to dry in a room where there were old things, and when they were already dry, he would organize them with scissors and put bunches in very small packages. Raisa, who at that time also lived in Medellín, helped him deliver them to the neighborhood friends who came and gave him money in exchange for the ground grass I'm talking about that Raisa and her friends like, including her husband Randy.

One of those days, when my dad was watching the news, they showed plants on television identical to Artur's, and my father got very angry. So much so that he went out to the backyard, tore them out, and threw them over the fence to a field that was behind our house, which is now not a field anymore but a very tall building where many people I know live and greet. My mom told me that because of those plants, she herself called the soldiers to take Artur away and turn him into a soldier like them. Some of Artur's friends, who also used to buy ground grass, were taken away by the soldiers and turned into soldiers, and they only returned to greet their moms, dressed as soldiers, with shaved heads. When Artur stopped being a soldier, he came back home already dressed like people who are not soldiers and... You know what...? He didn't want to plant plants to smoke anymore, he just drank aguardiente at parties with friends. Those friends of Artur are old like him now and are very good people. Raisa is also older, and I think of all those who smoked grass, she is the one who still does. I remember finally that everyone laughed, and I did with them when we saw that in the field where my dad threw Artur's plants, many plants like the ones he threw away sprouted, and all the dads from the Laureles neighborhood had to pull them out.

Surely, Raisa must know if a tiger is a man or not. Sometimes when my mom tells me that some animal is a woman and then Irina or Eleonora tell me the opposite, I feel like Hugo when the video game device won't let him win and he stays thinking, staring at the TV for a long time. It's the same. Hugo does it until he realizes that the device won. That doesn't happen to me because when the device is going to win, I already know it. Anyway, when it wins, I almost always say, *"Wha-at-the-hee-ellll?"*

I visited the zoo many years ago, like fifteen or twenty. However, when they bring me to Miami, I like to go back, because even though I know many of the animals, like the white tiger, who is a man, I take the opportunity to meet the children of the ones I already knew or others who hadn't arrived yet. The zoo is about an hour away from Eleonora's house in my brother-in-law Tomás's car. When Eleonora hadn't moved to the old house that she now has as a new home, we used to get there in about five minutes. Sometimes, I don't have to ask if an animal is a man or a woman because just by looking at it, I can tell. For example, in lions, the male lion has a big head, and the female doesn't, meaning the opposite of us, because in us, men have short hair and women have long hair. At some point, my brother-in-law explained to me that if an animal has hanging balls near the tutu, like me when I'm not cold, it's because it's a man. I thought about the tigers and saw myself trying to turn one over to make sure if it has balls or not. I've seen how tigers eat another animal bigger than them. What would happen if the tiger doesn't like me bothering it by looking to see if it's a man or a woman? I stopped thinking about the tiger and thought about other smaller animals like pigeons that poop on the railings of my house, and I got more confused because my brother-in-law told me that if it has balls, it's a man, and if not, it's a woman. I don't know what to think about the pigeons that don't have balls or tutus. Now that I think about it, neither do fish, frogs, lizards, crocodiles, snakes. It's so hard to understand. I think I'll have to ask Tomás again. Anyway, the most important thing for me now is to know that I'm a man because I have balls and a tutu, and that Amparo is a woman because I think —although I've only seen her in movies or when I'm asleep— she doesn't have balls or a tutu but beautiful boobs because you can see them above her blouse. In Medellín, there are people who resemble tigers or lions. Amparo looks like one of those long-legged red birds. I remembered her when I saw many gathered in heaps on the edge of a small pond.

"Wha-a-a-t's i-it na-a-me?" —I asked Raisa.

"Flamingos," she answered me. "Beautiful!" she added.

"Ju-ju-just li-li-like Am-paro... Me-e-ellín!"

"Amparo? Who is Amparo?"

"My gi-i-ir-rlfri-i-end, bea-eau-ti-i-ful. Um, Me-e-ellín!"

"Is she very pretty? Tell me, tell me!" she said because she didn't know about my girlfriend and got interested in her.

I tried to explain to her that she looks like a female flamingo; slim, with a pretty face like the Virgin of Santa Gema's church, and that even though I haven't seen her naked when she's real and not when I see her asleep, I imagine her as beautiful as the flamingos.

She paid attention and ran to tell Randy, her husband. Randy is a thin man, very tall, with hair that reaches his back. I think his hair is straight like Amparo's... Lies. Amparo's looks a bit curly, but very little. One thing that is similar between his hair and Amparo's is the coffee color, which when bathed in the light of a bulb, looks yellow. My sister's husband is a kind man who apparently can't speak like my parents because he only speaks English. I think that because it's Raisa who always helps my mom understand everything he says. Everything is so curious: Raisa helps my mom understand what Randy says, and my mom is the one who helps me understand what people say or helps me understand what people tell me.

They asked me to tell them more about Amparo.

I told them everything they asked, and I see that they enjoyed it. That is, for that moment, we were like those friends who walk and talk. They talk and walk, and sometimes they laugh. Like those in the movies where all the time, both the boy and the girl walk on a sidewalk or in a park, and when they walk, sometimes they look angry because he has another girl, or if not, because another girl is chasing him, or because she's the one looking at another boy, or maybe another boy is the one chasing her, but he's not as handsome as the boy she likes, or that she's the one who feels sorry for him because she thinks he's very ugly, like I think Irina thinks she is, or it's that she doesn't know how to comb her hair or doesn't take off those thick glasses so he can see her beautiful, or because she doesn't have a friend to help her comb her hair or take off those braces that make her look horrible. But a few minutes before the movie ends, they become happy, or they become happy again if they weren't happy, and then now she looks pretty, without the braces on her molars, or her hair messy, and they kiss, and they hug, and then they put on an English song that makes you sad, with the hairs on your arms standing, because then you imagine you're alone, or that you're still alone as you've always been.

In my own movie, I am indeed ugly. I am without needing to put braces on my teeth or thick glasses. I'm ugly because of my mismatched eyes, that is, by keeping one open and the other struggling to open because it closes without me wanting it to. There's no reason to put on glasses and make myself look ugly if I look ugly without them. If I put on those thick glasses, people wouldn't be able to see my eyes move like a dog's tail when it's very happy because I arrived or because Igor or Boris arrived. The truth is that we walked with Randy and Raisa like those friends who walk and talk, like those couples I told you about who, after being angry throughout the whole movie, make up and kiss and kiss and hug and hug and kiss again. They asked me about Amparo, and I answered them.

Randy bought ice cream for everyone. My mom didn't want any, but she did want water like my dad. When Raisa comes to our house in Medellín, which is also her house, I have to sleep in my dad's room so that she can have mine. From my bed, I can't hear my dad snore. She throws parties as I mentioned before, with many friends she brings from who knows where. I know many of them, but not all. The next day, my mom has to wash the dirty dishes, the lipstick-stained glasses, and even the smudged spoons left lying behind the plants in the garden. Sometimes, my mom throws those spoons in the trash and prefers to take out new ones from the old cupboard. There are many spoons there that people have given her for Mother's Day or her birthday, or because she thought of buying them supposedly to entertain her friends when they come over for drinks on weekends. My mom doesn't like her friends to see that she always puts the same spoons on the dining table. Surely her friends do the same when my mom visits them. Poor old lady. She also has to clean the floor from the cigarette butts that make the house stink and smell like the place where my dad and Igor play billiards with or without Tello. My mom ends up with aching joints because, even though the brown lady helps her, she still does extra work. Sometimes I help her, but Raisa doesn't because she doesn't get up all day. Anyway, she never did household chores when she was young and studying. Almost everything was done by Eleonora, who is the most responsible, and Irina, who also helped if she didn't have to go out to work.

I like Raisa's parties because initially, there are friends we haven't seen in a long time. Friends from when she was young and didn't dye her white hairs brown like she does now. But I stop liking her parties because they drink a lot of aguardiente and leave the next day when the bottles are empty, leaving the house a mess. My mom, my dad, and I can never sleep when she's in the house, so it's better if she always stays in London, as far away as a day or a night flying in an airplane.

I also have four or five white hairs on my head. Not as many as Raisa, and she dyes hers. But I don't mind. My four white hairs are nice, and I'm not old. If I were as old as my dad, I would throw myself in the trash. One day, I climbed into the trash can to see if I fit entirely. Luckily, I'm skinny and fit. Since that day, I think that whenever I want, I will throw myself in the trash. I'll do it when I get that crazy idea again because I don't want to see my mom's sad eyes. Remembering all this, while I was walking with Raisa, I decided not to tell her more about Amparo, and I distanced myself. That's when I approached Fausto, who was walking with my mom, behind my dad and in front of Igor, Anatoli, and Boris. Eleonora, Irina, the kids, and my brother-in-law walked far from us, although close to our gaze.

"Do you re-re-remember o-o-old fu-fu-fu-furniture, mom, ju-ju-just like m-m-mom's?" I asked Fausto, in front of where some enormous turtles approached to eat what could be bought in a machine to feed them.

Distracted, he answered, trying to pay attention, extending his arm so that the turtles would approach him but looking at me. He is very good when he talks because he never says bad things. I would say he is the best of all. We love him a lot because he is polite, he doesn't speak ill of anyone, and just like Eleonora and Irina, he loves us and looks after us, at least calling to greet us from Miami, Bradenton, or Key West during the week. Oh!... Artur loves us too because he does the same, although not as often. Fausto thought for a moment and, with surprise, it seemed he found in his head something about the old furniture. "Old furniture? Ah!... Yes... my mom told me," he said.

"I-I fe-e-el s-so b-bad, m-my m-mother is s-so s-sad," I replied.

I couldn't see if he liked my comment, and once again, I thought: 'Why does my mother get sad about that old furniture...? Could it be that she has something stored in it?' My mom always keeps things forever. Like her bed. She has never changed her bed. I, on the other hand, have a new bed that she bought for me supposedly so I could sleep better. She hasn't changed the drawers where she keeps the clothes, or the wardrobes, or the grandpa's paintings that always hang on the walls, watching us go up and down the stairs, that is, going up and down. Yes, that must be it. She is so used to that furniture that the last thing she wants is to throw it away. Uhmmm... all the things my mother doesn't want to throw in the trash are as old as I am. Could it be that my mother also thinks about me and doesn't want to throw me in the trash, even if I'm old? Am I becoming as old as the two of them? The pictures on the walls of my house have people who have never aged. That doesn't mean they don't get dusty sometimes. But that doesn't bother me because I clean them with a damp cloth, and that's it. Those people never grew old. How nice it would be to be like those paintings, especially my mom and my dad. How nice that they don't get older and have to die like everyone else.

I got sad again. Fausto noticed it. That's what I felt. It seemed that he was also concerned about that darn furniture. Just like my brother-in-law did when we went for a walk after I had that nonsense moment. He put his hand on my shoulder and pulled me close to him. He made me understand with words and gestures that old people get sad when they don't know what to do with the things they've had all their lives. Also, that the furniture has the same years as I do, and my mom is very afraid of dying and not knowing what to do with it. He clarified, mockingly, that my mom won't die on us soon, but in twenty, thirty, or forty years or maybe she'll never die for us. I remembered that Eleonora told me the same thing a few days ago, and I even thought that all my siblings thought the same. The old furniture thing already seemed sad to me, and I ended up saying the same thing I always say.

"'Tha-at fu-urnitu-ure, o-old ma-an, th-throw it in th-the tr-trash.'"

Once again, he made me understand that for old people, memories are as important as breathing and throwing memories away was not allowed for them. I remembered that a few days after Mrs. Gerlein's mom died, around the block, some old furniture was thrown away. They put them on the street, and the rain soaked them. I also remember that an old man passed by selling avocados, and he managed to take them in his cart. Surely, he doesn't have so many memories of his own, and he needs the memories that Mrs. Berta left behind, regardless of whether they were memories soaked by the rain.

We had lunch in front of the turtle place. Almost everyone ate hotdogs, even my mom and my dad. They complained, saying that the bread with sausage from Medellín is always better. That day, I sat close to Eduardito and watched over the stroller where Camila tried not to drop a piece of pizza. I love pizza and French fries.

In the distance, we could see the flamingos. I

watched them as we walked and rested. Amparo stood out among the most elegant ones. I imagined the neighborhood full of flamingos instead of people. The special thing was that all the houses were white, and the roofs were pink, and the windows and doors were black. It was very fun to see flamingos riding bicycles or motorcycles or Hammers or Cherokees. The old furniture came back to my mind, just like Fausto's words. I felt something very strange when I remembered that my mom cried for that furniture and not for me, Eleonora, or the grandchildren. Now, in my mind, there were flamingos, furniture, Hammers, and other mixed things. Anyway, if my mom dies or if I die, just like the furniture, they could throw us out on the street so the rainwater could soak us, and some avocado seller or the one who fixes pressure cookers or the one who sharpens knives or the one who sells dried fish could take us to his house because maybe he doesn't have so many memories.

"When Ha-ha-hammers ca-a-a-rs, whe-e-e-n?"

I asked my brother-in-law, feeling tired of seeing so many resting animals.

He promised that we would go later that day since we were on a trip. The rest of them agreed to go home to rest, especially my parents.

Every picture my brother-in-law took at that place told my lost smiles under the uncontrolled gaze of my eyes. Especially that day because of my happiness that was slightly crooked. I believe so. One of those days when you stay quiet and someone talks to you to make you speak or smile. Eleonora taught me how to distinguish happiness. I remember I was about twenty, and she still lived in Medellín. She told me that happiness is what I like and can't be eaten, can't be seen, but can be felt inside, and it makes you say or not say but think that...

—*I looove it...* or —*Thish iss sooo kool.*

I remember she first tried to explain sadness to me. According to her, sadness is something that makes me say or think:

"Wh-what a pi-i-i-ity, I'm sa-a-a-a-d, sa-a-a-a-d."

She explained that being a little sad is always better than being very sad, but it's better to be happy than to be a little sad. I could hardly understand her, but after hearing her many times, I understood that happiness helps sadness not be so boring, and sadness helps happiness not always be so cheerful. These pictures of me on top of beautiful cars told the happiness I felt so many times in a moment that lasted as long as a beer lasts for my dad when he plays billiards, from the moment it's opened until the foam drips down from the glass. Although the pictures always showed my absent face, I didn't care much because I was happy. I ended up thinking that happiness doesn't have just one face but many. Sometimes, it has a laughing face or other forms. Anyway, what I liked the most was that photo where I was leaning my butt on the front of the yellow Hammer, and another one where they sat me inside the car and told me to pretend I was driving. I felt like the one who drives the fantastic car on TV on

Mondays at eight. That Hammer is strong and smells new, just like Irina's car that seems new even though she's had it for months. I don't like my brother-in-law's car because it's old and doesn't smell new.

My dreams came true because they took me to that place where I also thought something I think when I'm in Medellín and walk to La Villa or Comuna Trece to greet Amparo: cars are like people. That's why I like to see them from the front and from behind. That's what I do when I see a nice car or when I see a beautiful girl pass by. In both cases, I think I would really like to be inside, driving. Cars always do what the driver tells them to without even saying anything. Sometimes, when the driver is angry or very happy, the cars groan with their engines and raise dust or smoke with their tires. When cars are hungry, they must eat gasoline. The same thing happens to me when I'm hungry at nine, twelve, or in the afternoon at six or seven. When I'm in my brother-in-law's car or in a taxi in Medellín, I compare them to people I know or have seen without knowing them much. There's a car that looks a lot like Caty, my house's dog. It's Irina's car. That Volkswagen with drooping ears that always seems to be afraid of other cars. When I scold Caty for something she did and I didn't like, she tucks her tail between her legs and looks like Irina's car. There's an old bus in Medellín that reminds me of Igor. It has a wide face, wrinkles on the forehead, and it always seems angry and tired of moving its big belly. I think that's because it's always full of people, and those people must weigh more now that it's old. My mom's body weighs her down a lot. I think her engine is not as strong as the Hammer's. When I'm on my house's terrace watching avocado sellers or those who sell cheese or fruits in carts or slow tricycles go by, I remember a little of my mom.

Lost in Coral Gables

I woke up when the sun was right above us. I knew because the garden plants didn't cast shadows when I peeked. My mom explained it to me when I was about fifteen, and I haven't forgotten it, unlike many other things I can't recall anymore. Since then, I more or less know what time I wake up. I woke up happy because I felt my gaze steady, without fluttering or that annoying flicker, but which makes kids laugh at Doña Emperatriz's, the owner of the iron grating store, where I go when the nights aren't cold and I feel like going. I also felt happy because I had gotten used to sleeping in without shame with everyone around. Even if they were awake early, they spoke softly or didn't speak at all to avoid disturbing my sleep.

I had orange juice that Irina squeezed for me and for the first time, I tried some pastries they called... *Be-e-e-g-g-g-g-ls-s,* which had soft cheese and everyone said were worse for gaining weight. In the afternoon, I went out jogging quietly not to attract the attention of those who get scared. Actually, everyone gets nervous, but my mom gets even more nervous because she thinks I'll disappear forever or for a long time. When I wake up like that, I take the opportunity to walk or run through the neighborhoods of Medellín. That day would be the third time I went out alone in Coral Gables, and my mom knew it. I took the same route as the golf course, step by step putting distance between us. I observed everything I stepped on and stepped on whatever appeared beneath me, being careful not to twist my ankles on seeds that looked like small mammee apple pits. I remembered Hilda, Berna, and Vincent's mom, two nephews she had with Igor, the oldest, who looks just like that old bus in Medellín that resembles him. I remembered her because she collects seeds, large dry leaves, and bits of branches to make flower arrangements she sells in her shop in El Poblado, and she once made them to decorate my dad's eightieth birthday party a few years ago. At home, they say she's the best at making flower bouquets in the whole world, and that's why they take her to many places and pay her a lot of money. I like Hilda, even though she's not my brother's wife anymore because he replaced her with a prettier one when the kids were little, and she's as pretty as before, or even more, but with some wrinkles around her eyes and yellow teeth from smoking so much. Hilda gets a new car every year, not like my brother-in-law, who keeps driving the same old Cherokee. I liked remembering her, even if it was just for a moment. Anyway, during my jog, I wanted to think more about Amparo than about her.

I jogged until I realized I didn't recognize the place I was in. All the houses looked the same, but none faced the golf course. *"Wha-at-the-hee-ellll?"* was the only thing I could say out loud because of the fear I felt, just like when we arrived on the plane. My stomach moved faster, and the pain wouldn't go away because of the fear of being lost. I needed to go to the bathroom, but I didn't know where, so I clenched my buttocks, hoping not to feel harassed. My stomach remained rebellious, and even though I knew that biting a lemon would fix it, I also realized I didn't have a lemon nearby. I needed my mom urgently, or the old man, or my brother-in-law. I turned back many times... about fifteen or twenty times until I finished the block to return to what I already knew. The more I ran, the less familiar everything felt. I didn't run anymore; instead, I walked, hoping to be near the golf course, or to see my mom's face, or to recognize Eleonora's old house. I thought that from walking so much, I could be in another place, who knows near what or far from what. No garden seemed beautiful to me, and I feared seeing giant squirrels with red angry eyes that would jump at my neck until it bled, like I did once to that fool who hit Professor Matilde. From the brush, I expected to see fears emerge. So, I preferred not to look at them, but my mind wouldn't let me. Fear is bad, my mom tells me every time I want to go alone to Villa, I mean to Comuna Trece:

"Aren't you afraid they'll rob you of your watch and stab you to take it off?"

Other times, she says"

"How scary. Those potheads have guns, and when they need money, they take it from people."

When I accompany her to the supermarket, we're always on the lookout for discovering fears within people. There are fears that are real, as they are dressed in fear like the potheads, like the beggars or... like the kids at the traffic lights. Thieves who wait for the elderly to get distracted to steal their money at the supermarket are fears that resemble people who are not so scary. Yes..., people like Artur, Irina, Eleonora, Fausto, or my brother-in-law. From a very young age, I named fears because I can't express them in words for my family to understand. So when I talk about them, I call them...

— *Kwai-it Strayn-jers.*

Kwai-it Strayn-jers is a good name for fears. When someone who is not a cop has a gun, it's bad. Every time I walk with my mom and see someone I don't know how they are, I ask her:

—*"Kwai-it Strayn-jers?"* And she answers yes or no, depending on whether she's scared too.

Lost in Coral Gables, I think I was scared, or rather, I think I got frightened. It's complicated. I feel fear when I think I won't see Amparo again because I'm scared of losing her. I feel scared when I think my mom might be gone because I'm afraid of being alone.

—*"Wha-at-the-hee-ellll...?"* *"Wha-at-the-hee-ellll...?"* I said again, realizing the mess I was in for going jogging alone. I shouted while I cried without tears, but with all the fear inside me, like when I cry in Medellín because my mom is taken to the hospital because of the lightning strike on her head. I walked all day until a darker color appeared in the sky, like every day when all the houses start to light up to make the trees not look so black. I kept my eyes forward not to look sideways, and I passed by the same places again. It was very hot, even though it was already night. A few, not many, passed by me walking or jogging, but they didn't even look at me. That's how people on the streets are in Miami, Medellín, London, or anywhere else I've seen them pass by. They see, but they don't look, and when they do look at me, they prefer to move away with a strange smile, bewildered because they can't find a face like theirs on mine .

I had to go to the bathroom because I couldn't stand the pain in my stomach. I did it next to a tree that was already dark because there were no lights nearby. Nobody found out because in that place, it seemed like nobody found out about anything. Anyway, I felt embarrassed because it was the first time I did it, and worse, because I got up without cleaning my backside. Many cars passed by that irritated my eyes, my right eye, with their lights. I would have liked to close them, but I wished more than ever for my brother-in-law's Cherokee to appear, no matter how old it was. I sat in front of a house five times bigger than ours. It had a long driveway that led to the door where two lights shone on each side. I felt confident sitting there because they couldn't see me from inside, thinking I was a *Kwai-it Strayn-jer*. I stayed there for a long time, I don't know how long. The night got longer. Fewer people passed by, and fewer cars too. Desperate because of the mosquitoes that kept biting my arms and legs, I decided to walk. I did it for a long time until I saw   a lit street, although it was far away. It was a street with some passing cars and buildings of different sizes lined up in front of a very high and thin bridge where the train passed. I liked seeing that bridge because I remembered when, on one of those outings to buy things with Eleonora, she told me about that bridge. When I asked her, *"Wha-at's diss caw-ld?"* she said it was the metro, the train that takes people to work. She was surprised when I told her it was just like in Medellín.

The truth is, the Miami metro reminds me a lot of the one in Medellín. When I mention Medellín, I couldn't help but think of my mom and her old piece of furniture. I never thought I'd disappear before that old piece of furniture. Surely, she would be mortified. She might think I died of hunger or was swallowed by some giant squirrel. I think she thinks about those things because here, in Miami, so many people vanish and end up lying around, dead, because the *Kwai-it Strayn-jers* shot them. My brother-in-law mentioned something similar when we walked on the golf course the same day he said the stupid thing. He told me it's calmer here than there, and people don't kill just to see someone fall dead. Some do, but they're very few, and that's why they wanted me to come live here, supposedly so my old lady wouldn't worry so much. Imagine, so I wouldn't get lost... and I am lost. Old people die when you get lost; they die of sadness. I say that because I could tell from the lady who owns the store down by Ochenta's roundabout. She faded away after her eldest son, Pedro, disappeared one day. One of those days when people leave home and never come back. They don't come back because... something happened to them. For example, a car ran them over because they were drunk at Don Quijote's roundabout, or because some *Kwai-it Strayn-jer* took them, or because they appeared dead somewhere, in some field, and no one knew what happened, or because they just vanished and were never heard of again. That's what happened to Pedro's mom. She died of sorrow a few months after they found Pedro dumped in a field, covered in flies, hands tied behind his back, and a hole in his head. Those days were very sad for my old lady too; she knew Pedro's mom and dad. I'm sure my mother fears for me every time she sees me leave the house. She tells me stories like Pedro's or others who have died, like the guy from the store downstairs, near the women's school, to whom some *Kwai-it Strayn-jer* asked for a pound of sugar, and when he turned to get it, they shot him in the back, and there he lay dead. I found out about it before my mom did. In fact, I was the one who told my old lady what happened. I was walking that day when I saw a smoking motorcycle speeding out, furious, and then I saw people going into the place and a lady who was his wife and came out screaming. I knew it when I saw her. She was shouting, "they killed him, they killed him." I walked faster, and when I was in front of the place, I saw the guy lying on the ground, face down, with a pound of sugar in his hand, although the bag was torn, and the sugar spread all over the floor, soaked in blood, sweet blood. That day my old man told me to go home because maybe the *Kwai-it Strayn-jer* would come back to shoot more or to see who was around to shoot later. So I did. Things like that have happened in Medellín.

For example, not long ago, Hilda paid us a visit. I'm sure my mom invited her for beans. She visited us in her new car, and when she was getting out of the car, which Vincent was driving, someone put a gun to her head and stole her car. I remember I was on the terrace, looking at the usual stuff. When I realized what was happening, I got very angry and went down to help Vincent so they wouldn't take his car, but he controlled me himself so they wouldn't shoot me. That Vincent is very weak; he doesn't fight to keep his car from being stolen, that new car of his. Anyway, they bought another car later, a red one, the same "Nissan" brand. I know because I write it down every time I remember or when I'm playing around with how many car brands I've learned to write.

So I wouldn't go out alone, and because my old lady is very afraid when I do, she tells me:

"Take care, my boy. Remember what happened to Pedro. Remember how his mom died of sadness because they killed him." I just tell her:

"Yeh, yeh, yeh-hh."

Sometimes I say it angrily, and sometimes not. I say it because I'm already grown up, and grown-ups like me go out alone, angry or not, especially when we have a girlfriend, like me with Amparo. I have her regardless of the fact that she has other boyfriends who hug her, kiss her, and even touch her. I say it because I've seen her boyfriends touching her butt and tickling her, and she gets upset, but I pretend not to see it. I pretend because it makes me sad and angry, and then

I go out and walk back home very slowly, watching the buses pass, the taxis pass, the motorcycles pass, the thieves looking for something to steal, and the old folks figuring out how not to get robbed. I walk carefully, making sure no car, taxi, or motorcycle runs me over at Don Quijote's roundabout or on some street full of people, cars, and dogs looking for food, also watching out so nobody steps on them or kicks them to get them out of the way. I cross the streets running to avoid getting run over by a car, running but very sad because of her. Amparo doesn't know she's my girlfriend, but I do. My mother worries a lot that I might get lost in Medellín or that I might show up, dead or alive, but sick, meaning with a broken leg or blood in my stomach or back. That's why I've never gotten lost. What my mother didn't worry about with me in Miami was me getting lost, like now, that I'm lost in Coral Gables, far from Medellín. In Medellín, I know how to get back home, no matter if it's day or night. But it's not the same here. So many houses with so many trees look so alike that now I can't differentiate one from another. They're all equally fearful, although beautiful. In Medellín, the streets and houses aren't as similar as they are here, and when you get lost, you ask someone...

"Where is Laureles?" And that someone tells you:

"Over there, or here, or just around the corner..." Because there are people on the streets, always. Not like in Coral Gables, where there are only houses that seem uninhabited, cars that seem to drive themselves, and no one else.

'When you're the one who's lost and don't know how to get back, then there are two dead people: the one who got lost and the one who stays. Like Perucho's mom, who stayed but also died. Of sorrow, but she died. Like many moms in Medellín whose children disappear and never return, or if they do, they come back in one of those black bags that are thrown in the trash. Now my mom worries about the furniture and about me at the same time. For her, the furniture must be dead just like me,' I thought. 'My dad, on the other hand, probably thinks I'll reappear and won't end up chewed up by a giant squirrel, but hunger will take care of me.'

I'm already in the lit-up place. The streets no longer have trees or the squirrel-faced fears. They look more like square shadows or shapes moving in the darkness. I compare these fears with those of Comuna Trece and didn't know which ones I preferred. Anyway, I think fears are fears and there are no better ones because they're always worse. The roofs of the building entrances invite me to rest. Many in Medellín do the same; they sleep on the sides of the buildings, tired of walking, like I am now. I nestled in many of them, curled up, hoping to see something that would calm me down. Some individuals or small groups approached me, walking towards me without knowing I was there. I didn't dare make myself visible. They would surely talk to me, or they would get scared, and I wouldn't understand why I never understand those who talk to me for the first time. I also feared they would speak to me in English, which would be worse for me because I would have to guess twice. When they got close, I shrunk to make myself smaller. I think I saw many people pass by before falling asleep for a while and waking up with my leg cramped. I had no idea what time it was, although there was no one around anymore, just a car passing in the distance and the sounds of cars taking people to the hospital. I fell asleep again until someone moved my body.

"—*You-uuu Kwai-it Strayn-jer,*" I said, frightened and harassed again by the daylight.

In front of me was an old woman, not as old as my mom, well-dressed, with a thin jacket the color of the flamingos from a few days ago. Although her face was smiling, I was afraid to look at her. So I huddled, putting my head between my legs, but still keeping her figure in my eyes, which, due to the shock, moved like a ping-pong ball. Around me, some people looked at me puzzled, just like Hugo when his video game doesn't work, and he finally realizes it wasn't plugged in. How funny Hugo is. I always plug in his device for him so he won't be so confused. I think the old woman who shook me had a sad face, just like others around her. They spoke to me, but I couldn't understand them. I didn't even hear what they were saying. I only saw them. They chatted among themselves, seeing my scared, fearful, or perhaps embarrassed face. I sat down and lowered my head to avoid looking at them and listened to murmurs, lots of murmurs. Someone in the crowd approached me, offering me coffee in a McDonald's cup. I knew it because, like the old lady, he touched my arm, and when I reacted, I saw what he was offering me. He was a young man like Fausto, but taller and hairier. I didn't know if he was just as nice. I thought he was because he offered me coffee without asking for money, just like Eleonora, who never offers me coffee, supposedly because it makes me crazy, but she gives me milk, water, or orange juice. My brother-in-law sometimes gives me his beer. I recognized the coffee from its smell, like the one my mom makes in the mornings or in the afternoons when her friends visit to talk about things that make them laugh or make them cry. When they talk about things that make them laugh, I assist with my laughter, even though they look at each other not to laugh more. But when I hear them cry or wipe their eyes, sometimes tears come to my eyes, but I don't let them see me cry. They're probably sad about things that happen in Medellín, like the death of a friend or a son. My mom's friends are old like her and almost always talk about someone who died or was killed at the farm, downtown, or somewhere else. Many times, they cry more than they laugh. When the older ones die, the less old ones will have gatherings to drink coffee and laugh for those who haven't died or cry for those who have. I accepted the coffee eagerly and without looking him in the eyes, I said, *"Th-aa-ngk yoo!"*

He stepped away without understanding that I thanked him for his coffee. I drank it in sips while they looked at me and tried to talk to me. With their persistence, I said the same thing I said to the policewoman at the airport when she asked my name:

"I no talk Eeng-lish."

She didn't understand, and they all looked at each other, making signs of being confused. I silently chuckled inside because I know this happens to anyone who doesn't know me and hears me speak. The difference was that I didn't have my mom nearby to explain what I meant, so I fell silent again. The old lady took my hands, inviting me, but I recoiled, hunching my arms and tucking my hands under my armpits. After a while, she insisted. I felt cornered, maybe embarrassed, scared, or afraid. I couldn't distinguish. So, I decided to leave with the coffee in my hand, making sure no one was following me.

I walked a couple of blocks and sat on the curb in front of a place that caught my attention because people of all kinds were going in and out. I saw parents, moms, and children; beautiful and ugly women; young people like Amparo and old ones like my dad. Seeing them coming in and out, I assumed I could do the same, so I entered. It was a bookstore with a second floor reachable by a round staircase with twisted green iron railings. I liked it; it was very pretty. I like stairs that go up because they invite you to discover other things. Apparently, in that place, people helped themselves because there were no staff members asking if you needed assistance or anything similar. I liked that because I didn't want anyone to talk to me. In Medellín, someone always comes out saying,

"Need help? I'm here to help you."

I observed the books in front of me, especially those with drawings and photographs. I liked one about new cars, and I memorized it. There was the yellow Hammer, where I was photographed a few days ago. It was so much fun. I also found a magazine about video game devices that reminded me of Hugo. I wondered, 'What is Hugo up to?' He must be riding the bicycle his mom sent him from New York. I also thought he might be knocking on my door to come and play with me, but since I'm not home, he would return to his house, where he lives without his mom. I thought it would have been better if Hugo had come with us to Eleonora's house, so both of us would be lost. I chuckled at the thought. I might have been thinking about Amparo longer than I thought about the Hammers and video games.

I wonder what Amparo is doing. Is she riding in her boyfriend's Hammer today, or is she hiding to avoid getting caught in a stray bullet in Comuna Trece? I wish I were lost in the Comuna because everyone knows me, and they would have taken me home.

I caught sight of a round clock on the bookstore wall that said it was eleven. I assumed it was eleven in the morning because there wouldn't be light if it was nighttime. I decided to go back home for lunch. How stupid I felt when I remembered I had been lost since yesterday. I felt desperate again, and my stomach rumbled loudly. I was hungry, very hungry. I realized that books don't satisfy your hunger, so I left thinking of my mom. I knew she would be very sad not to have me around. I remembered the old lady who held my hands earlier, inviting me, and I walked, hoping they would give me coffee again.

I arrived quickly, and although there were no

people, I settled in the same spot. From there, I saw a McDonald's and walked towards it. I spent a long time watching from the window what was happening with those who ate a lot of hamburgers. I was afraid to go in because I didn't know how to get one. I looked at the ground, hoping to find some money, but there was nothing on the ground. There were only a lot of chewing gums stuck on the pavement; they were already black with dirt. I imagined my dad going to the bank to get some money for me, and I also imagined myself buying a hamburger with the money my father gave me.

A family had noticed me in front of the window; I think they were scared to see my face and my evasive, uncontrolled glances. I smiled at them, just like I did with the airport policeman, remembering my mom's request. They pretended not to see me, especially the parents, and continued eating, but the kids started making faces at me and sticking their tongues out. Sometimes the parents scolded them, but they kept teasing me. I'm used to kids making fun of my face, so I kept looking out the window. The hunger was getting unbearable, and I was about to burst. My head hurt as much as when I wake up with that nonsense that makes me shout at my mom...

"Yoo're uh bich, I'm tie-urd. Bich, bich... I'm ve-ry ang-gree."

I watched people putting fries, barely touched, in the trash can. They did it without any remorse, and there I was, watching them. Watching them like our dog watches us when we're having lunch in the dining room. The skinniest ones were the ones who threw food away because the fatter ones ate it all. I decided to go in and take whatever I could from the trash if I could grab something. I did it because I couldn't stand it anymore, and the nonsense was lurking around. I also put a glass with some Coca-Cola between my elbows. I felt no disgust or shame because when things are already in the trash, they have no owner, and then they can be mine, or a dog's, or someone dressed in fear like me that day. I had never been so hungry as to eat what others had left in the trash. My mother wouldn't have let me, nor would I have attempted it.

I don't think anyone saw me do it because people never notice if someone is rummaging through the trash for what others throw away. At least that's what happens to me. I sat not far from there and ate as much as I could find. Now, I wanted to wash my mouth as I always do after every meal, so I went back to the bookstore that seemed familiar. I went to the men's restroom and tried to clean my teeth with toilet paper smeared with soap. It was really bad because I almost vomited, but it stopped being bad when I put the water in my mouth, and finally, the bubbles stopped coming out. I also splashed water on my face with a little soap and in my hair so it didn't look so messy. I came out again, determined to return to the place I came from. To that place full of trees and big houses where squirrels run on the light cords. I remembered places I had visited many times. My head felt happy again when the highest part of the hotel my brother-in-law showed me appeared in my memories. I was very happy just thinking about how good it would be to see it in the distance, even if it was only the tip. I remembered the name I learned and said it out loud:

—"Ho-te-ee-ell Bil-mo-o-org-g."—

I've only been so happy once before. It was the day my mom came home from the hospital. 'Now, how to find the Hotel Biltmore if I was surrounded only by very beautiful houses and trees as big as the whole world?' This time, I didn't answer myself, but I thought and thought. I thought as I walked through blocks that looked so much like the ones surrounding the golf course. Again, I felt tired, thirsty. I feared having to go back to that roof under that building to sleep because it was far away. I cried again without tears, and the desire to find my way was fading away like when TV shows end before new ones start. I reached a small grassy area where there were three big trees, similar to the ones always in front of Coral Gables houses, and I lay down to look at the sky while thinking about things that didn't let me think about how to get back.

My head felt happy again when my eyes saw the topmost part of the tree. It occurred to me that from there, I could see the hotel my brother-in-law showed me again. I thought of movies where ship captains climb up high to see if they find land that isn't water. I was very happy just thinking that I might see the highest point of that hotel from a distance. So, I climbed up the tree with fear or maybe with terror, perhaps terror because I thought I might fall like a seed or like a coconut. But the desire to see the hotel was too great, so I didn't care much about falling while trying.

I started climbing, grabbing the biggest branches. I hadn't sweated a drop on my forehead for many days. That was because Miami's heat was making me sweat. While climbing, I got distracted when I saw a nest of little birds. How beautiful they are! I would have liked to be a bird to see the Biltmore from afar and end this nonsense of looking for it. There were many birds in that tree, and they got scared when they saw me. I'm sure my face looked strange to them too. I also saw squirrels, many squirrels, running away or hiding behind branches when I scared them, although they didn't hide completely; they peeked their faces out while moving their tails. Things look better from Coral Gables trees. At one point, I felt I was in the middle of that tree, and the branches below me no longer allowed me to see the ground, and those above me didn't allow me to see the sky, and those in front didn't allow me to see ahead. I assumed those behind wouldn't let me see behind either. I felt lost again, but now inside a tree. I felt a little bit of laughter for feeling so sad. Now I was lost inside the tree without knowing what to do. I rested for a while, watching beautiful animals, especially squirrels playing. After a few minutes, my head felt happy again when the highest part of the tree appeared in my memories, from where I could see the hotel again. I was happy again just thinking about how wonderful it would be to see in the distance, even if it was just its tip. So, I climbed higher and higher, not looking back, or down, or forward. Slowly, I saw the blue of the sky through the branches, although I still had to climb higher. I tried to find strong branches, but at that height, the branches weren't so strong. Again, I rested, looking at the sky through the branches. I saw a strong branch disappearing in front of me, and I carefully followed it, crawling on it. At one point, I saw the bridge where the Miami metro passes, and I recognized the place where I had slept. I recognized it because it reminded me of that wide corner I passed by on my way to the bookstore where I washed my mouth with soap. I recognized the buildings lined up in front of the metro. I felt good for recognizing them because at least I could go back to them. Anyway, I looked around, wherever the branches allowed me to do so.

After a few minutes, I found myself staring at the roofs of the houses around, just like their yards and pools. I like pools. Eleonora's old house doesn't have one, but I'll ask my brother-in-law to build it. What a pity for Eleonora not having a pool in her house. I enjoyed seeing the houses from above, like in an airplane when it's about to crash, and the roofs become vast. I wanted to see the hotel, but I couldn't find it anywhere. I felt sad again. I supposed it must be on the other side, so I decided to go back the same way on the branch. The wind rustled the branches, scaring me. I looked down and felt my legs frozen with fear of falling. I think going down is scarier than going up. I remembered being in Puerto Aventuras when my brother-in-law and I climbed the tallest pyramid. I mean the pyramid the Indians built that's in all the pictures talking about Mexico. I can't remember its name because it's very hard for me to learn; I never knew how to say it. I also didn't learn to write it down like I did with other places like Miami, Key West, Bradenton, or New York, where Anatoli. That pyramid was the tallest of all, very high and old. It was where they killed the Indians who misbehaved. That pyramid was so tall that people below looked like dots on paper, or better yet, like fleas on a dog when they move within its fur and when you see them, they've already seen you first, and they run to hide so you don't pinch them and make their bellies full of blood burst.

Remembering what happened to me on that pyramid, I wanted to climb down, but I couldn't. I remembered when that day my brother-in-law had to ask people to help me descend, carrying me like a little child, because I was scared out of my wits. Because fear kept me from moving. That day, I felt scared all day long, and it only went away when I finally agreed to take the pill from my mom. Sometimes, when I'm scared, the last thing I want is for my mom to give me the pill. Usually, I take it when hunger doesn't let me be. It was like today, lost on top of a giant tree, very scared, not moving, gripping the branches, even with my teeth. But now everything was worse because I didn't have my brother-in-law or the people who carried me that time nearby, and the pyramid didn't move with the wind like the tree did.

The wind became stubborn one more time, making me even more scared. I cried without tears, looking everywhere, waiting for something to help me. I remembered Priest Pio's mass and the Baby Jesus. My mom tells me that the Baby Jesus helps me when I need him. So I said forcefully:

"Whe-e-ere ah you, Bay- bee-e Je-e-zus, whe-e-ere ha-ve you gone?"

But the Baby Jesus was nowhere. I called him again and again. Nothing happened. I stayed very scared and sad. I don't know if I was more or less scared than before. I stayed there suspended for hours. I liked being there, watching everything happen from above. I looked at some girls playing in a pool at a very big house. I saw them tiny, but I saw them. I got distracted watching them play, splashing water, and sometimes staying still, sunbathing their bodies. It seemed to me that one of them took off her top and sunbathed her breasts. It seemed to me because I couldn't be sure. They were very far away. Anyway, I thought it was true. I saw it in my head, regardless of whether it was true or not. I kept staring at her, hypnotized, like when I see it on television. Although her breasts weren't visible because of the distance, my tutu straightened up. I looked around, and no one was looking at me, so I let it straighten until it made me shiver. I felt a little embarrassed in front of the squirrels, but they didn't say anything. No one else knew, no one. Just like when it happens to me in Medellín at night watching movies.

Afterward, I felt very calm, nestled between two branches, watching and forgetting everything that was happening to me.

Time passed, maybe a few hours, when I thought about going back. I was hungry again. I climbed down carefully, branch by branch, for a long time, maybe an hour or more. The heat was terrible, even though the tree branches protected me from the sun.

When I finally jumped to the ground, I looked up and congratulated myself. I did it because I was very high. I had never reached such heights before. Never. But hunger haunted me again; it haunted me.

I went back the way I came, and again I saw the bridge where the Miami metro passes. I walked hurriedly and settled back in front of McDonald's, watching what people ate, or better... what people left. Then, in one of those moments, I went in and picked things from the trash again. This time, I did it thinking of the crazy ones who do it in movies, crazy ones who have no home and nothing to eat. I went out with my hands full, just like in the movies, and sat down to eat on a sidewalk. I ate until I was about to burst. I was very happy to do it. I thought that if my parents didn't find me, I could live like this, eating at McDonald's, sleeping at the entrance of some building where an old lady would wake me up the next day, and a guy similar to Fausto would give me coffee. I also thought I could even sleep in that tree, accompanied by the squirrels and little birds that, even though they go to bed at five, would keep me company so that I wouldn't be sad. The idea of wanting to stay sleeping in the tree came to me because from up there, I could see those girls I liked again. Maybe from above, I could see them again.

Determined, I went back to find Eleonora's house. I did it for several hours until I found myself again by the tree. The giant tree. I climbed to rest on a fork. It was the second time I did it that same day. I felt like those leopards that climb trees to rest and even stay there sleeping so that lions or hyenas won't bother them. I did it because I liked that tree. I slept for a long time, I couldn't tell how long. When I woke up, I felt like never coming down again. I climbed up to where I thought I had reached the first time. At one point, the wind moved some branches, and there, very, very far away, I saw the highest part of the hotel. My head became happy again. This time much happier than when my mom came from the hospital, smiling and with her cheerful look. I was so happy that I let go of the branch and started running. I was so foolish because I rolled and rolled until something from the tree stopped me. Nevertheless, my happiness was greater than my scratches. I climbed back up the branches and confirmed that the Biltmore was there, even though far away, and I thought Eleonora's house must be close to it, waiting for me. I knew I had to walk and walk to at least get to the golf course, but I didn't care. Now it was just a matter of getting down from the tree slowly because the slip left my arms, legs, back, and belly scraped as big as my whole body. I think I spent an hour trying to get to the ground, but I did it.

I walked, thinking I was heading toward the hotel, and after a few minutes, I felt like I was on the edge of the golf course and saw the Biltmore Hotel, smiling at me. This time, I cried with tears, but without sadness. I walked a little more until I arrived at Eleonora's house, where no one was. It was strange because there were already sixteen of us at home. I decided not to move, and I sat on the front steps. It didn't take many minutes before I saw the Cherokee driven by my brother-in-law and my mom in the passenger seat. Everyone jumped out except my mom and dad, who waited until last, just like when we arrived on the plane until it was their turn to hug me. I was very happy, although I feared that my happiness might trigger that condition that makes me feel like a devil and attack my mom with words like the ones Boris says or that I say when I'm like that. However, that condition wasn't inside me. Apparently, Baby Jesus had won, and he was inside me. I hugged my mom and dad so tightly that I can't remember ever doing it like that in my life. Everyone was talking to me, but I didn't answer them because I didn't know what to say. After a few minutes, four police cars arrived, and some of my family members got out. Two large cars, like the ones that take patients to the hospital, also arrived, along with other cars with long tubes similar to the ones used to broadcast news on television.

As if they had agreed, they left my mom in front of me. She looked very serious and confused. I knew it because she wiped her chin with a kitchen paper. She asked me tremulously what she asks me every night when I come home from La Villa, I mean, from the neighborhood, and she's already confused by my delay: "What happened to you, son?"

— *"He g-g-got l-l-l-lost. R-r-r-running, he g-g-got l-l-l-lost!"*—I stammered.

She hugged me deeply, making me feel her thick body and her labored breathing. My dad, quiet and very serious, hugged both of us. That's his way of loving me: without laughter and silently. A policeman who was talking to Eleonora approached my mom and said something to her. I noticed my mom nodded. Then the policeman approached, and I smiled at him. Some men dressed as doctors did the same, just like on TV when, before the end of movies, the injured ones appear with them by their side or pushing hospital beds on wheels. There were two of them in green shirts and pants, with a device hanging from their neck that they put on one's heart and say, "Breathe in, breathe out." They said something to Eleonora, which she must have told me. Then they brought a stretcher on wheels, just like in the movies I just remembered. Eleonora asked me to lie down there, but I resisted because I wanted to go inside the house. She begged me to do it until I did. They looked all over my body and even shone a flashlight in my eyes and touched my bones. The scrapes hurt.

"It h-h-huurrts, a looottt, a looottt!" I said to Eleonora.

She explained my pain to them, and then they gave me a pill with apple or grape juice. That's what I assumed from its color. However, I looked into Eleonora's eyes, who understood and without asking, said, "It's apple juice. The one you like."

A lot of people who had arrived in front of my house watched from behind a yellow tape that the police put up so that no one could pass. Also nearby were a lot of people with microphones and television cameras. I remembered the movie of the monster on a bicycle in the air, the one with a long finger that turned red without having been hurt. After a few minutes, they took me in one of those cars to a hospital, accompanied by all my family. I stayed there for two days until I came back home. Upon entering, I imagined Amparo waiting for me sitting on the couch where I sleep, reading a newspaper with my picture on the cover. I think it was because I got lost and now I've reappeared. My mom still doesn't know what happened because, even though I've wanted to tell them, I haven't been able to, and even though we've tried, they still haven't been able to find out. They'll never know what happened to me. I understand it will be that way. One day, I'll ask Eleonora what that newspaper says about me. I preferred to keep imagining Amparo. Then I saw her in my head, mockingly asking me:

"Did you get lost in Miami?" I answered yes, raising my eyebrows.

She smiled and ruffled my hair. I like it when she does that.

About Things That spoke

They talked about the same things they talked about every afternoon. Sixteen of us were there, silent: Camila, little Eduardito, my dad, and me on one side; Anatoli and Igor didn't speak either, they just listened. Sometimes, Camila drew attention when her drool-covered, chewed-up toy fell. Eduardito and I occasionally asked for something, but we didn't distract anyone. They believed, as they always do, that I wouldn't be paying attention. I rarely do because I find it boring to hear things I sometimes don't understand. But that day, I understood everything since I woke up. When I wake up like that, understanding, seeing, and even speaking become easier for me. I took the opportunity to find some blank sheets of paper and a pen, to sit very close to them and do what I always do when I'm alone and listening. I drew eyes with long eyelashes, numbers from one to ten after nine, and wrote the name of each person in my house, including Amparo's. Then I wrote down the car brands I like. I wanted to do it without making mistakes, looking at the catalogs we had chosen during our stay. By those days, the Hammer was no longer my favorite car; it was one that is spelled like this: l-a-m-b-o-r-g-h-i-n-i.

I liked that car because it looks like a wasp, although it has a fierce bull in its name. I don't like the Hammer as much anymore because it looks like a beetle to me. My brother-in-law promised to take pictures of me when I learned to pronounce it correctly. For now, I call it:

—*Ambi-i-i-i-rgin.*

They said things related to the old furniture, which I retained to ask about later before going to sleep, as my brother-in-law was never around when they gathered to talk. Raisa once commented:

"In London, it's not very expensive to have it because Randy is from there."

At Raisa's house, there are things from the painter grandfather. Things that appear in the green book that everyone flips through when they arrive at mom's house. My grandfather painted a lot, I think now that I'm forty-four and see that people remember him more often than I do. I only remember him when others remember, looking at his paintings and I'm there. My dad has many of the grandfather's paintings, like fifty or thirty. He has them hanging on all the walls. Anatoli, on the other hand, has many that he took without my dad's permission when he travels to Medellín with the two Irmas—his daughter and his wife from New York. Raisa does the same when she comes from London, with or without Randy, her latest husband. Irina has a painting by my grandfather that my dad gave her as a gift in Bradenton, one of those days when we were invited to visit her. It's a painting of a skinny woman, just like her. With hair as long as hers. Whenever I've seen that painting, I think of her. Maybe that's why my dad gave it to her? Perhaps my grandfather painted it while watching her pass by. Eleonora, on the other hand, doesn't have paintings by my grandfather. I mean, she only has a few small paintings. As big as half of my hand, and she says they're not so beautiful. I think when my parents die, everyone will fight over my grandfather's paintings. Not me. I've known my grandfather forever, like I've known my mom and dad. I saw him paint while drinking aguardiente and listening to church music. How boring his music was… I like reggaeton. Grandfather never wanted to be my friend because he scared me when he painted to prevent me from ruining his paintings. He would call my mom when he took me to his house. He did it by shouting:

"Anastasiaaa… Ludovico went up to the studio. Take him away, please!"

And my mom would send Fausto or Boris to scare me away. When they came to get me, I kicked them in the shins so they wouldn't take me down, but they ended up giving me a smack that hurt more than the kicks I gave. I knew my grandfather wasn't my friend because he would see me coming and wouldn't greet me like my friends do when they say:

—*"Hello Lu-do-vi-i-i-ico!"*
And I reply:
—*"Wha-a-at's go-o-o-ing on?"*
They still recognize my grandfather even after he died. I know this because I see several books with his paintings at home. I'm not sure if after I die, they will talk about me as the painter grandfather's grandson or as Ludovico, the one with the fast-moving gaze, or as the fool of Mrs. Anastasia, Mrs. Oslo's wife from Laureles. I just know that when the old folks die, if they die before me, I'll remember them as my companions every day, who only told me some things like "open the door for your dad; open the door for Hugo, he's knocking; tell your dad that the food is ready."

This year, Raisa made something like a calendar out of paper to mark the days and months, adorned with my grandfather's paintings, and she handed it out to her friends during this trip. She also brought one for Eleonora, Irina, Anatoli, Igor, and Fausto on this trip. I can't remember if she brought one for Boris. I would like to be friends with grandfather now. Too bad when the old folks die, they stop painting.

What Raisa said intrigued me, and I tried to find a way to ask her something by getting closer.

"You, Lo-oo-ndon, wh-wh-when?"

"I'll be leaving in a week. Would you like to live in London?" she asked me.

I heard everything she said, but I was left wondering what she had really wanted to tell me.

I made an attempt to understand by squinting my eyes, but I couldn't. While I squinted, the others were waiting for my answer. I saw them looking at me, eager for me to answer yes or no, but I was just trying to decipher their words. This time, it was Irina who helped me understand her question. When I realized what she was asking me, I thought about London. I thought that I don't even like London a little bit. It's gray and cold like my quiet and anxious days, like Hugo's days, which are so much like mine. Besides, it's where, everywhere, there's a picture of the old woman with hats who lives in a very large house with a very large clock, who not only appears in the photos every day but also on television. Sometimes, when I'm in Medellín and watch TV, I also see that old woman from London with her hats. What a bore that old woman is, and I already have two at my house, or three if I count myself. I thought about it and wanted to tell Raisa, but I figured that even if I tried, she wouldn't be able to understand. I decided not to and answered, hugging my own shoulders the way people do when they're cold:

—*"Lo-oo-ndon iz so tie-re-sohm! Soooo cooold, mee cooold, verrrry cooold."*

Raisa smiled at my response, but she didn't seem happy. She clapped her hands once and raised her eyebrows as if to say it wasn't her who did something wrong and said, looking at my mom:

—"You can travel with him to London and

accompany him while he gets used to being alone…"

My mom got sad again. It was already many times that I had seen her like this during the visit to Miami. Despite my mom's sadness, they remained silent, very worried, looking at me. I was confused again and really wanted to approach her and make her laugh.

"*Lo-oo-ndon mee?*"

"Nothing, honey, she replied. We're talking about the old furniture."

"*Wi-ch wun?*" I asked.

—"The old furniture, kid… Don't you remember?"

"*Ah! Ye-ah, ye-ah, ye-ah, I remem-ber. That ol' furn-iture, for, um, tr-ash.*"

She laughed, but it was a fake laugh. The others did the same, and then they looked at each other again and preferred to hide their faces, that is, their gazes. I was left feeling the same as when someone explains something to me that I don't understand in the end. I went back to the table and continued painting the letters of the cars. I heard other things, and I assumed they also had to do with that darn old furniture. The things my family talks about turn out to be very strange to me. Like the furniture they have been talking about for many days. Once, when Eleonora came to the United States, all that was talked about at my house was the boyfriend who stayed behind in Medellín because of her. It took a long time for them to stop talking about him and start talking about my brother-in-law. That's why I say that when my family starts talking about something, they do it for several days; they do it until they get tired. Now that I mentioned it, I'm remembering the days when David, Eleonora's boyfriend, used to go out with my sister because my mom had finally given them permission to go out. I remember I always had to go with them. They would buy me cotton candy, and they would leave me at the theater watching a movie and eating my cotton candy until the theater lights turned on. Sometimes, the theater lights turned on, and they weren't around. I would get anxious, and they would show up. David is now a man with children and works selling car-related things. I got used to stopping by his store to greet him, but I stopped doing it when I found out that Eleonora didn't like him as much anymore, but liked my brother-in-law in the United States more. I started feeling bad for David when he asked me about Eleonora, and I didn't know what to tell him. At that point, my brother-in-law was more appealing to me than him too. I think David missed my sister Eleonora as much as I miss Amparo now. It's possible that David still misses Eleonora. Only he will know. Going back to the conversation I was trying to guess that day, this time I heard something that caught my attention and surely had to do with that darn old furniture. Suddenly, Fausto said:

—"The problem is that I live alone... he'll get bored, and I won't know what to do..."

He said, looking at Raisa, and made a gesture of not knowing what to do either, raising his hands and eyebrows, just as she had done earlier. Then he said again: "The only thing I can do is give you money to help…"

From what I noticed, my mom didn't like what she heard from Fausto because she pressed her lips together. She pressed them so hard that her entire face tightened. Then I saw her sad again and a little angry. Or rather, not so angry. Worried, and maybe serious. My dad, on the other hand, neither said yes nor said no to what Fausto said. That is, he didn't say anything. My mom was the only one who dared to talk to ease her face.

"Not money!… What he needs is love, like the love I've given you since you were little."

Who knows what my mom meant. I would have liked to know. I felt a strong urge to stop being an idiot and join that conversation, but that has been impossible for me. It has been impossible because I am someone who can only watch what others talk about, nothing more. I am someone no one tells anything to… Nothing serious. I am someone who is answered with silly things when I'm interested in knowing. I am someone who is answered without even thinking that those answers sadden me and make me feel so nonsense each time. Things I ask full of intrigue, full of curiosity; things that are answered with any joke that I almost never understand, but which I laugh at and serve so that I don't ask more. Everyone in my house and everyone on the street has always believed that what little they answer me and what little they talk to me is enough for me. They don't know that I need their long, dedicated answers. Answers that, because they are long, should bore me to hear them and that I might have to say:

"Ah, so tires-s-s-some, all this chit-ch-ch-chat."

Anyway, I noticed my old lady's eyes shining differently than they ever have when she's sad. For example... how they shone when Grandma Tasha, my grandma, my mom's mom, died, or when Grandpa, the painter, passed away. The gleam in my mother's eyes that day was different. Everything was just very strange. Honestly, it was the first time I had started thinking that an old piece of furniture was so important to everyone, and apparently, it meant even more to my mom on those days. Not that the piece of furniture was alive or anything. I don't believe a piece of furniture could be so important that everyone in my house would do nothing but talk about it and my mother would suffer because of it. Unless that old piece of furniture moves without anyone pushing it. Like how I move. And it gets hungry every two hours like I do, and it has a girlfriend like Amparo, and seeing her makes it happy every day. I can't imagine that piece of furniture being in love with a table or a dining chair, for example, and being liked by its friends, the paintings hanging on the wall, the mirror, or the clock with big numbers that greets it every time it sees it. Thinking about that, I remembered the movie where toys come to life when the real child isn't looking. How funny they are. They play when the child doesn't see them. If they played when the child does see them, I'm sure they would enjoy it more. Now that I think about it, surely all the furniture in my house is like children's toys, who play when no one is looking. Is that why sometimes, when I sleep, I hear some noises around? It must be because some foolish piece of furniture stumbled and fell. How funny. Furniture also stumbles and falls like old folks going to the supermarket who occasionally trip and fall, and people laugh, just like they must do with the furniture. From now on, I'll think that furniture is alive, but it doesn't move when someone is near. They probably eat, cough, and cry. And they get lost trotting around Coral Gables. Poor things. When they come back, no one will know why they got lost. That happened to me.

Come to think of it, if the furniture weren't alive, it wouldn't make my old lady and my siblings so sad, or me, who gets sad seeing that my old lady isn't happy. Surely, among themselves, they take advantage of the chaos and do good or bad things, without anyone noticing. It's not strange at all that they pretend to be ignorant, just like we do when we need to pretend. Like me, when I'm hungry, I go into the kitchen and without my mom noticing, I stab a piece of meat with a fork that wasn't meant for me but for old Oslo or Boris, and I eat it almost without chewing. If I chewed, my mom would surely notice and scold me. When my poor old lady realizes the meat has disappeared, she asks, very sternly, shouting from the kitchen:

"Who ate Oslo's meat?"

So, I act like I don't hear it, like it's not me. And when she asks me again, looking me in the eyes, I answer:

"Me-a-at? Nah, me no 'member."

Pretending to be ignorant is easy. At least for me. For example, when I go out, I act like I don't know and shout to my old lady from the gate:

"I g-guh-oh ruhn too La V-vil-lah."

The truth is, I'm pretending because I'm not going to the Villa, but to the Comuna Trece to see Amparo, my girlfriend. When I visit her, I stretch my mouth, eager to give her a little kiss on her cheek, but she pretends not to notice and moves away as if she hadn't noticed I was trying to kiss her. Anyway, come to think of it, she has never let me kiss her cheek when I arrive or when I leave because she's very discreet, that is, she pretends not to, so she doesn't have to say anything, like she doesn't like me to kiss her cheek to greet her or say goodbye. How strange. Sometimes, when someone arrives and I'm close to her, I see how they kiss her cheek or mouth, and she doesn't pretend not to notice like she does with me.

Furniture pretends not to notice so no one blames them for what happens, or for what people passing by do, or for what the dog does when it passes, or when the turtledoves pass by, who sometimes pretend not to notice and enter the house to eat the crumbs from the floor that the dog hasn't seen yet or maybe has seen but prefers to pretend not to because she's not hungry.

That's why I think furniture is the one that notices the most about what happens. They notice silently, without even blinking, without complaining or saying anything. One thing I'm sure of is that they never tell lies because they don't talk and pretend not to notice, so they never say things as they are or as they're not. Besides pretending not to notice, they're very sharp. One day, when I had this foolishness going on, I was in the living room, and I kicked the mahogany piece. It didn't say anything. It endured everything, even the pain, because I kicked it hard. Think about it; if my foot hurt, imagine how much I hurt it. But it endured and didn't even rub itself. I say it's sharp because at that moment, still in my foolishness, I decided to close a drawer that had half-opened because of the kick, and the idiot ended up smashing the big toe on my right hand. It makes me laugh when I think now that that day my big toe on my right hand hurt, and my big toe on my right foot also hurt, which became swollen and purple because of the huge kick I gave it. Luckily, both don't hurt anymore. That piece of furniture hurt me, but at the same time, it pretended not to notice, as if it hadn't been or as if it hadn't even realized.

When I return to Medellín, if that plane doesn't fall apart fighting with the wind, I'll wait until everyone is asleep and try to catch the furniture doing things. I'll hide, or better, I'll pretend to be asleep so they start having fun, and when they least expect it, I can scare them, making them jump. It's very likely that now that we're all in Miami talking about old furniture, the furniture in my house is out there smoking a cigarette with one leg leaning on the wall or crossed, and sitting on another piece of furniture, like a chair, for example. It's not strange that they're having a party today; they surely learned it from Raisa. That's right. They must be doing the same thing Raisa does when she shows up there. One thing I'll do when I get home is check if the walls have furniture leg stains. And if the stains are mahogany, it's because the mahogany furniture, where my mother keeps the glasses Fausto sends her, stained the wall accidentally.

"Now, if the stain on the wall is red, for sure, the one leaning was the red table," I said, emphasizing the word 'red.'

It was the red table, tired of standing still on its four legs, that decided to lean for a rest. At least, when I'm very tired of standing, I lean against the wall and lift one leg as if not to get so tired. That table is where my mom sits to talk on the phone and where she keeps notebooks with everyone's phone numbers. I would say it's not a table but rather a seat that resembles a table because it's low and only serves for my mother to place her behind and sit there talking for hours. Poor red table, it has had to endure so much over the years.

I hope I never find out that any of the furniture was there dirtying the walls because I would scold them, even if they pretend not to hear me. Speaking of the red table, I now realize that it's the only one that knows the truth about what my old lady talks about on the phone. Surely, she knows very well about Hugo's things. I mean things that maybe even Hugo himself doesn't know, but my old lady does. Or my things. Like, for example, things I do every day, but I don't consider important, and she does, and they make her happy or sad, like when I wake up without the foolishness and more talkative than other days and wash the dirty dishes, or when I feel like petting the dog and telling her things I saw on the street. How much will the furniture in my house know about me? Now that I think about it, it's very possible that the old piece of furniture they're talking about here knows many things about me. Like, for example, that inside it, in a place no one knows, under all the drawers, I keep the magazines of naked women that I've been given in the commune and that I have to bring home in my pants. I hope that piece of furniture never tells my old lady because I would be very embarrassed. Do furniture move at night when they feel everyone snoring? Do they take advantage when I'm not around and look at my magazines? Speaking of snoring, everyone in my house snores except me, because I've never heard myself snore. It's been many years since my old man doesn't sleep in the same room as my old lady, I think because he snored first and woke her up before she started snoring and woke him up. When at night I hear them snoring, I know very well when it's him and when it's her. I'm tired of thinking about furniture that moves when you're not there. That's why I want to go back to what they were talking about in Eleonora's living room, while the furniture pretended not to hear.

"If they give me the money, I'll take care of it," Boris said, emphasizing the word 'if.'

Usually, when Boris speaks, no one pays attention. This time, everyone listened because they looked at each other, widening their eyes as if what they had heard was very, very bad, or very, very good. I don't know that for sure. Because Raisa replied:

"Ha… if he drinks what he doesn't have… I better keep quiet!"

Apparently, Boris didn't like Raisa's comment at all. He got angry. Very angry. He stood up with a red face, wanting to devour it alive. He pulled out a handkerchief, wiped his nose making a lot of noise while cursing, who knows what. The others laughed, covering their mouths as not to do it too hard. I also laughed seeing all of them, only I didn't cover my mouth. He left the living room towards the bedrooms, cursing out loud:

"These are the things that drive me crazy!"

That ended their conversation that afternoon. They also went inside the house, and I didn't see them gathering to talk anymore. Apparently, they didn't want to because talking about an old piece of furniture isn't funny at all. So, I decided to look out the window to find things to entertain myself. I had gotten used to doing it in the few days I had been at Eleonora's house. I like staring out the window because it's like when I stand on the terrace of the house in Medellín for a long time. I see the girls from Sagrado Corazón school passing by. I see them because they're pretty and charming and because they're not old like my dad or most neighbors who are as old as him. There's a girl I like a lot who has been passing by since she was as little as Eduardito. Now she's grown up, like Amparo, only darker, and she has black hair like Eleonora's, but curlier. I like watching her pass by, even if she doesn't know I always watch her. I've never wanted to go down and see her up close because I think she wouldn't like to see my eyes.

One day my dad was looking for the warmth of the sun that reaches the terrace to dry the towels or the clothes my mom washes and sends me to hang because she never goes up to the terrace due to the pain in her ankles, knees, and other things I can't remember now.

"That gir-r-r-rl's so pret-t-t-ty," I said, looking at my dad and pointing with my finger.

"Very pretty, son... very pretty," he replied.

He fell silent. Then he looked at me and smiled, tilting his head back. I liked that. I thought he might talk to me more about that girl or other pretty girls. I've always hoped my dad would talk to me about pretty girls.

I devoted myself to watching her pass by, as I

always do whenever I see her walk by. I like it when she arrives because I see her face always without sadness. Perhaps because I see her from above. When she passes under our house, I see her head with a line in the middle and her hair falling on both sides. Sometimes the line of her hair goes to one side, and on other occasions, the line is not visible because that day she preferred to braid it and fasten it with clips or ornaments, almost always white, like her skirt. She always passes by in her blue uniform. The part I like the most when watching her pass from above is that her behind moves while her legs walk. That day I got so excited that I wanted to tell my dad that I like that girl. That I like it when I see her pass by. But my dad wasn't there anymore, and I hadn't realized it. So, once again, I found myself alone with my happiness. Yes, with my happiness. That thing I like and that can't be eaten, that can't be seen, but that is felt inside, and that makes one say or think, *"I luh-luh-love it, it's re-really coo-cool."*

I also like it when I see her fading into the distance. When she is very close, I don't think about Amparo, but when she disappears, Amparo becomes my happiness again. Now I'm sad because I don't have them close. Neither Amparo nor the girl whose name I don't even know.

When I point my eyes far away, like when I see that girl getting farther away every day, I notice that my eyes don't move as much as when I look into someone's eyes who is talking to me. That's why I like to look into the distance. That day, at Eleonora's house, I kept looking into the distance. I waited without haste for something to appear in the distance. Perhaps a squirrel fleeing from something that scares it or approaching something it likes, or some bird of a new color or some weird shape in its feathers... And that it jumped from a branch to the ground or from the ground to a branch. I looked in silence, although I didn't stop hearing my siblings talking, laughing, or occasionally bursting into laughter, as they had been doing since they arrived in Miami. I kept looking while I licked a soursop ice cream stick I found in the fridge.

Because of the burning sensation I felt in parts of my body, especially in my ribs, I remembered when I rolled among the branches because I ran from the heights of the tree, scraping myself all the way down to my bottom. The burning sensations from those scratches were fading, but some still bothered me. Nineteen days had passed since we arrived, and apparently, the trip was about to end. Outings to Miami were not as frequent anymore. Now, the gossip among everyone was more repetitive and lengthy. Watching them talk all those days, I also noticed that the more they talked, the more they turned to look at me. It intrigued me because this time they looked at me differently, as if thinking about me while they stared. I can't explain it. How funny it was when I thought that now that I'm forty-four years old, I'm even more foolish than before, and that's why they look at me so much. I should have figured that maybe that's why they were looking at me. I don't understand why I've become so foolish. I wish I were less so to not worry my old lady. Surely, she thinks that because of my foolishness, I'll get lost when we return to Medellín and I'm walking through Comuna or La Villa. That's what she must be thinking now that I got lost in Coral Gables, convinced that I'm grown up and that I won't get lost anymore. How absent-minded I was!

I realized that my mom has looked at me the least, but that didn't bother me much because I know she's the one who has always been most attentive to me throughout my life. She doesn't look at me very often because she knows I'm always there. There where she always thinks I am. There where she imagines. The same thing happens to me with them. I don't have to look at them to be calm that nothing happens to them because I know they are always there. They will always be close to me, even if they have died of old age or exhaustion from not looking at me. If my mom doesn't look at me so often, my dad does even less. He doesn't even talk to me. Well, almost never, because when he feels that Hugo is with me because he came to visit me and play video games, he approaches my room's door.

— "When is this boy going back home?" —he asks.

— *"At ni-i-igh, in de eve-nin."* —I reply.

—"What a shameless boy! He should be at his home and not come here to bother us so much," —he goes away saying.

Hugo listens and looks to see what I say, but since I don't say anything and just shrug my shoulders, he continues playing videos. It doesn't bother us anymore when my dad gets mad at Hugo.

I liked the ice cream so much that I went back for another one. I was no longer ashamed to do it at Eleonora's house because she always told me that the fridge was mine for whenever I wanted ice cream, milk, cake, or whatever. This time, I chose a mango ice cream and went back to the window where I wanted to keep watching. I noticed a strange silence because everyone fell silent at the same time, and they gave me some glances when I passed by them. Anyway, I smiled at them, saying, *"Th-is i-i-ice crea-am is-s s-so-o-o co-o-ool."*

And I kept walking. When I got to the window, I wanted to remember what I was doing before going for the ice cream, but I couldn't remember. I assumed I was there for a reason. Finally, I saw the squirrels and realized I was following them just like the birds. This time I thought about myself. How strange, I never think about myself unless I'm hungry or cold, or sleepy after watching television until three in the morning. I thought about myself and the lady who helped me when I got lost and the kids who made faces at me at McDonald's. I would like to find them someday, greet them, and tell them that I appeared and that I don't have that fear anymore. Maybe I could live like this when the old folks are no longer there. I had to swallow saliva and feel how my eyes welled up and how my nose started running because of thinking about the sadness of feeling that the old folks might die before me and that they feel sad about leaving their old furniture.

The squirrels didn't entertain me as much anymore, nor did the cars passing by every hour, nor the old people dressed in bright colors that appeared and disappeared trotting, nor the giant trees in each house on the block, nor anything. I was alone, thinking about myself, lost in Coral Gables, in London, in Medellín, in Chicago, in New York, or in Bogotá, where I was taken before coming to Miami.

Since my permission to enter the United States was no longer valid, they took me to Bogotá supposedly to get it. I remember shivering all the time and no blanket helped me feel warm. That day, we stayed at a hotel as cold as the city itself. The best thing was that we were attended to by Hernán, a friend of Boris who serves coffee, orange juice, and meals on the red planes that travel from Colombia to Miami or other places far from Medellín. Hernán is very good. I like him because he is quiet and kind. More than Boris, more than Igor, and something like my brother-in-law or like Fausto, Eleonora, or Irina.

Speaking of Hernán, once we traveled to London, he was working on the plane that took us. He was very special with us. He offered us food twice and lunch twice. He brought me lemon juice every time I wanted lemon juice. He brought it to me so that I wouldn't get so much stomach pain because of the ride on the plane.

That Hernán is very good. When he arrives in Medellín from Miami, he brings us gifts from Eleonora or Irina. Small things like some soft shoes for my dad or my mom or some belated birthday gift from a few months ago. Hernán also greeted me like everyone does, but with a cheerful smile.

— *""Hello Lu-do-vi-i-i-ico!... Ho-ow are yo-o-u?"*

— *"Heeelllo, bu-u-ddy."*

— *"Ho-ow are yo-o-u?"* he repeated.

— *"O-o-h! Goo-ood."*

That trip to London was very good. We could sleep all night. The bad thing was that because of the nap, my mom's hair got messed up, making her embarrassed in front of other people, who, although they had slept like us, didn't have messy hair or a mouth smeared with dry drool. She never gets up and goes to the supermarket without bathing, brushing her teeth, combing her hair, and putting on the perfume that makes me sneeze. My dad doesn't go out disheveled either, and even less me. For example, today I'm wearing shorts, knee- length. They are Medellín's police color, not Miami's, as Miami's police officers have uniforms of various colors, not like those in Medellín, which are the color of trees. I also have a white shirt that smells like the soap from the bear in the box. I have white socks that aren't visible because they are very small and some sneakers of the same police color. Sometimes, when I visit Amparo, I wear new things. I usually like shirts that say things on the front or that have painted drawings

like Mickey Mouse or Pluto. When I visit Amparo, I wear an old watch so that it won't be stolen, and I never wear the chain with the Baby Jesus. My mom tells me that I should only wear it when we go out together to eat mondongo in Poblado. We go whenever one of the three of us has a birthday. We do it to celebrate, even if we are alone and receive calls all day.

How tiresome that everyone calls us to congratulate us for being older. Last year, when it was my birthday, I didn't want to pick up the phone even though my mom begged me. I was furious about that nonsense, although not as much as the one I had these days. I didn't want anyone to remind me. Only Hugo or Amparo. I remember that I went to Amparo's house wearing a blue shirt and checkered shorts. She was inside, and although I knocked on her door, she didn't come out. Or rather, her little sister came out, the one who makes faces at me when I go.

—"She's busy, making lunch!" she told me without me asking.

—"*Te-e-ll he-e-e-r III'm ha-a-avinnng-g a-a bi-i-i-irthda-a-ay.*"

I didn't see that she understood me. I think she didn't even want to understand me. She put her fingers in her mouth and stretched it to the sides, sticking out her tongue. She turned into a devil and went inside like that, slamming the door. She always does the same. I never know if she tells Amparo that I arrived or if she doesn't tell her, and she finds out only when she goes out and sees me. As always, I sat in front of the house on the sidewalk, leaning against a lamppost. Meanwhile, I remembered when I was as small as that devil and went to the door when Irina or Raisa's friends came and also put my fingers in my mouth and stretched it to the sides, sticking out my tongue. Now I see that I looked horrible making faces at those poor people who stayed outside when I slammed the door on them. Sometimes, when I was a good brother, I told them that someone was waiting outside. But when I wasn't a good brother, I didn't warn them, and the poor ones had to wait until someone else came to the house or left.

I waited that day for that girl to be a good sister and stayed alert. However, Amparo didn't come out. I noticed several times how that little pest stuck her head out of a window and made faces at me. Almost all the kids make faces at me, except for my nephews. That day Amparo came out late and greeted me when she saw me from her door. She came out upon hearing a man offering avocados. She waved at me from there and stayed talking to the avocado man. She looked at me and said goodbye with the same hand she greeted me with. Then, she turned her body and closed the door. I had no way to tell her it was my birthday, and she never found out. Anyway, I liked seeing her come out with her hair tied up, just like the ladies do when they do the housework. I decided not to think about her anymore because I didn't want to be sad. I paid attention again to some things that entertained my family, like that damn piece of furniture. "In this house, he could have another room for himself," this time I heard it from Eleonora.

I thought it was good that this piece of furniture would stay in a room in her house, where it wouldn't get damaged. Eleonora is very diligent. Her single bed, which still waits for her in our house in Medellín, is the same. It's still as beautiful as when she hadn't married and was David's girlfriend. Surely my mom will be happier because Eleonora's old furniture lasts a long time. I liked seeing how the issue with the furniture would be resolved, making my mom happier. I only worried that once my mom 'resolved' the matter with the furniture, she wouldn't care about dying anymore, and I would be left alone with my dad, who doesn't know how to cook beans, roast arepas, wash clothes, or buy groceries. If my mom dies because she doesn't care about her memory-filled furniture anymore, then I'll have to ask Amparo to make lunch and breakfast for me. I think maybe I'll have to learn to do it for myself and my dad. I'll ask Eleonora how to make beans so they taste like the ones my mom makes. If I don't solve it somehow, I'll go back to McDonald's.

About the Elderly in Bradenton

From seven in the morning, the sky created new colors that turned dark and threatening. They were reddish-purple colors. Purples that turned into bright grays that darkened quickly. Earlier, around two, Irina invited me to a place where she buys clothes and other things every time she visits Miami. Sometimes, they invite me when they don't want to go out alone. They've always done so since I turned eighteen. Before that, it was my mother who forced me to go out with them, anywhere, supposedly so they wouldn't be embarrassed to be seen with me. I guess I was quite stubborn before I turned eighteen, as they've let me know. When I visited Irina in Bradenton years ago, I noticed she lives in a very calm place with many elderly people and very few children, lots of birds and very few cars, a lot of silence and very little noise. It's a place where it's too lazy in the morning, at noon, and in the evening. It's a place with many more elderly people than me, more like as old as my parents.

She told me that many elderly people there no longer wanted to live where they were young. She meant they didn't want to live in places like where

Anatoli lived. She was referring to New York, where the cold scares them away, much like it scared me away one December, or because they got tired of being young and just wanted to sunbathe their stomachs while reading books by the poolside. The elderly in Bradenton are the elderly who have already made a lot of money to pay for their elderly things. Yes, just like all the elderly. My dad also made money to have his elderly things, even for my mom to have her elderly things, and even for me, who, although not elderly, still have my things without having to sunbathe my belly while looking at books I can't read! I like to see books that have drawings like those of Donald Duck or SpongeBob or books with new cars or books with beautiful women with or without clothes.

Every time I take out the garbage at my house, I think about the elderly people in Bradenton. It happened to me this morning when I saw Eleonora throwing it away. She threw away things she no longer needed, like clothes with buttons that fell off from being fastened too much or that were left to sleep in when the pajamas weren't clean. The garbage always waits there, lying down, without haste, until the elderly people get even older. When the elderly die, they go to the people's garbage dump. They go there asleep. Or rather, they take them there when they're dead. When Bella, my dad's older sister, died, we all went to throw her away in the garbage, dressed in black. Even the children went with us or were taken because they can't go alone. What seems strange to me every time there's a known death is that, instead of putting them in a plastic bag, the kind you get from the supermarket, they put them in a box similar to the wooden furniture my mom doesn't want to throw away. I've always been clear that when people die and are thrown away, they always go in furniture that replaces the plastic bag. Especially when the one who dies is someone known, and both the children and friends get sad because they died. I'll ask my mom what color she'd like her furniture to be. Well, when she dies. Later, I'll ask my dad. When I die, I want a red piece of furniture with the same glass window they made for Bella's furniture. I'll ask to be thrown away in the garbage with the video game console and the last Mario Bros game. Sometimes, when the *Kwai-it Strayn-jers* people die and they show them on TV, they're thrown away in black bags. I see that every day at seven before my mom's soap opera. In Medellín, many people are thrown away in black bags. That's because there's no one to claim them. My mom told me. One day she explained to me that the *Kwai-it Strayn-jers* people go out on the streets to rob or kill, and when instead of robbing or killing, some policeman kills them first, then nobody knows who they are, and they're thrown away in black bags.

My mom tells me that elderly people die of old age, but Eleonora told me they die for many reasons. I don't understand the difference between dying of old age and dying for many reasons like coughing or the flu. My mom always goes to the doctor for medicine so that she won't have pains that might kill her. When she talks to her friends, she says:

—"When my time comes to die, let it be sudden, without pain."

I'd like to know what she means by... sudden; I understand what painless means. My mom gives my dad a tiny pill every day, supposedly so he won't die from heart problems. Now I'm really confused. What does dying of old age have to do with dying from the heart or suddenly? What does the pill have to do with all this? I've always understood that the pill is taken so that one doesn't do something stupid. Surely dying from the heart or suddenly are other kinds of stupid things that happen to people. I think elderly people who still think, not like some elderly people in Bradenton, know that they're becoming like my mom's furniture or like those clothes that lose their buttons, and they also know that someday they'll leave some house, turned into garbage.

Irina told me that one of those elderly men is laid down by a lady on one of the long pool chairs, and the elderly man doesn't move at all. I hadn't noticed until one day she showed me. She told me that that man no longer spoke, saw, or understood. So I kept looking at him from the apartment window overlooking the pool where all the elderly people come to read books all day. Since that man caught my attention so much, I watched him for several days. I assumed all elderly people were the same, but I never imagined that there were so many who no longer spoke, saw, or understood.

One morning, I saw them arrive. He was sitting in a wheelchair, coiled up like a tire. I realized he didn't even know he was there. Something similar happens to the garbage bags in Medellín or Miami or Chicago, because they're already dead since they're garbage, and they don't know they're there. Because garbage also can't hear, see, or understand. Those who truly hear, see, and understand are the ones who throw away the garbage. A brown-haired lady with tired eyes, wearing a hospital uniform, pushed the wheelchair. The lady was quite thin, although tall. I noticed it was very difficult for her to get the elderly man down and place him in the chair by the edge of the pool. I wanted to help her, but I felt far away because I was only observing them from Irina's apartment window, which, although facing that pool, still has a fence separating us. I think that elderly man got tired of wondering what would happen to him when he got old and preferred not to think anymore before arriving in Bradenton. Apparently, not many people visit the elderly in Bradenton. It seems the same happens in my house, as my parents are rarely visited by those who went to the United States or London, like Eleonora, Irina, Fausto, Artur, Igor, and Boris, not to mention Raisa. Now that I think about it, I'm the only one in my house who visits my parents every day. Who would believe it, when elderly people need us the most, that's when we leave them alone .

Irina told me that when Christmas comes or when they're told that the elderly person has died, some relatives go to visit them. Someone has to take care of throwing away what the deceased left behind, including the deceased themselves. Most leave their books smeared with pool water or mementos like my mom's furniture that might interest the avocado seller.

One thing I liked about the elderly people in Bradenton is that they all greet me and smile at me. Well, those who still hear, see, or understand. Except for the man in the wheelchair, who doesn't smile or greet anymore. They're kind and don't pay much attention to my eyes or the shape of my face or the thinness of my legs. They're kind because they got tired of being young or being like those people who do things not very well done. Like those children from McDonald's, like Amparo's sister, or like some of the ones from the Comuna who kill just to mock the dead. I know because I saw it once when, after a fight, they laughed at the one who lost because he died with blood in his stomach. I saw it in La Villa before traveling to Miami, but I didn't tell my mom.

For moments, I doubted if I had always been an elderly person. I doubted it because I've never worked like everyone else works when they're not elderly, nor have I studied like everyone else studies when they're young. But I also thought that I'm not old because I walk very fast and play video games. I calmed down even more when I thought that neither the elderly people in Bradenton nor the ones in Medellín play video games like I do. They only know how to play cards and read, and I can't do either.

Although I had admired Irina's Volkswagen since she arrived at Eleonora's house, I had never ridden in it even though she had invited me many times. Truthfully, I hadn't ridden in it because I heard Artur say it was a car for girls, and I didn't like that.

"Dis car-r i-i-ss fo' ma-ns or wo-o-maans?"

—I ask very seriously when she invited me. She didn't understand, so I repeated.

"Come on, Ludovico, I know how to drive well!" She invited me again, looking puzzled.

"I'm a ma-aan' na-a-wt gay," I replied.

I responded and understood why she understands me as much as Eleonora. She understood it better because I said *"gay."* I say it every time I see a man doing things like a woman, such as cutting women's hair at a salon or getting their nails done, or putting on lipstick, or eye makeup, or plucking their eyebrows like Eleonora or Raisa. She burst into laughter and ran to hug me while still smiling. She asked me why I thought that car was only for women. I told her that Artur said it one day while talking to my brother-in-law and I was listening. After explaining that the gray color of the car's pot is also a color for men, I got in.

It was a beautiful evening because I spent time with her. She loves me a lot. I know because of how kind she is to me. When she offers me juice or milk, she gives me a soft paper to clean myself in case I get dirty. When she takes me to a restaurant, she explains the food they sell and helps me choose what I want. Not like my old lady, who orders what she thinks I like without asking me. Irina lets me choose, especially the sneakers I like for jogging or the chocolate ice creams, or the pizza. The last time I was at her house in Bradenton, we went to the *Pier-r-r-rg*, at least that's what I call it because she made me repeat it many times. She says it better because she says it in English and also because, unlike me, she can speak well. I can't say it even in Spanish because in Medellín, there is *"no Pier-r-r-rg,"* and I only know the one in Bradenton, which is said in English. I mean that place that goes into the sea and fills up with people to watch the sunset. It's a long wooden path. When you reach the tip, you see the beach, and it's as if people are walking on the water. Many people go there every evening to see the sun disappear behind the water, while many people catch fish from the sea or take pictures, smiling, or making faces so that when others see the photos, they laugh. What a pity for the fish. They are idiots for getting distracted watching the sun like everyone else and letting themselves be caught. How silly they are. If they didn't look at the sun, they would still be alive. I think some days Irina goes there alone because she lives alone. She has always lived alone. Since she lives in Bradenton, she's becoming like an old lady. Well, because she likes to watch the birds and the lake behind her apartment where there are small crocodiles and also signs telling those who play golf not to let themselves be eaten by them. Her apartment is nicer than my house in Medellín. It's clean and pleasant, without pigeons that poop on the railings or avocado vendors, or newspaper sellers who wake you up with their shouts. It's a place like the ones that appear in magazines. From what I see, she buys a lot at the supermarket to get furniture, fake plants to decorate every corner, and clothes for every day. Not like Eleonora's house, which is old, and its walls are falling. What a pity for Eleonora. She doesn't have a new house or a new car, but she does have real plants.

When I'm in Bradenton, I miss avocados and beans. I also miss the joy of the people. I like it when those around me are cheerful because it rubs off on me a bit. In Bradenton, I feel lonely, even though Irina is close. There are people who seem to be happy feeling sad. I think that could happen to Irina. She lives alone, far from all of us, without friends and without children. Far from the world and only close to herself. Not like Eleonora, who taught me what it means to be happy. I would like to ask Irina about her happiness, but I can barely say to her:

—*"Wha-a-at's go-o-o-ing on?"*

… She wouldn't understand me… I'll never know how to ask her. Since I was very young, I got used to not asking her. Maybe that's why I've never had that nonsense because of her. Yes…, that nonsense that makes me so mad. When I have it, it's because I forgot something or because my mom didn't like something, or my dad, or because Boris ate something that was meant for me when I came back from the street. What I don't like about Bradenton is that very early in the morning, the lawnmowers at the golf course wake up the old people. What the mowers don't know is that they not only wake them up but also us.

"Which one looks better on me?" Irina asked me while bringing a blouse to her face, one with small red flowers and another the color of the sky when there are no clouds. Everything looks good on her because she is slim and pretty. I always tell her:

"I l-like b-both, th-they're n-nice. Wh-which one d-do you l-like m-more?"

She insists that I tell her which one, and I end up pointing to any of them. Then, she buys it and wears it the next day. I like seeing her in the clothes I help her buy. She asks me if I have a girlfriend or if I'm hungry, or thirsty, or... what I'm asking Baby Jesus for in December, or what I want for my birthday. That day, I told her about Amparo. I said I want to go back to Medellín to see her again. She asked me where she lives. I answered in the Villa. I had to lie again, just like when I lie to my mom because if I tell her that Amparo lives in Comuna Trece, then she tells my mom, and she gets confused. She also asked me how old she is, and I said very young. She asked me if she's tall, and I said one hand taller than me. She asked me if she has siblings, and then I remembered her little sister and told her no. We talked a lot about Amparo, although not as much as I talk with Eleonora. I've always felt I talk easier with Eleonora than with Irina. Maybe because Eleonora is younger. Almost as much as I am. Maybe that's why I like her more. I prefer accompanying Irina rather than her accompanying me. In my house, there are some who entertain me more, that is, those I like to spend more time with. That doesn't mean I don't love them all. Because I do, even though sometimes they annoy me. The truth is, there are some I do like to be with. For example, I really like my mom to accompany me whenever I accompany her. As for my dad, I prefer to accompany him because I feel he doesn't enjoy accompanying me for too long. Perhaps he does, but I've never noticed. As for Fausto, I don't like him accompanying me entirely, nor do I like accompanying him. I just like seeing him and greeting him sometimes, and other times, I prefer to greet him but not see him. That's because he rarely looks at my face and talks to me. He just limits himself to saying...

—*"Hello Lu-do-vi-i-i-ico!"*

I see that Fausto likes to live away from the family. It's as if someone is chasing him or as if he doesn't like anyone knowing something he has been hiding for many years. Whenever he wants or needs, he prefers to come to see us. He prefers it rather than us going to see him. Every time Fausto comes home, he comes with a new friend. Fausto doesn't have a girlfriend, wife, or children. He has very nice dogs, white with black freckles, like the ones in the animated movie. Fausto is very strange; he is a very good person, perhaps the best of all. Because he is a good person. We all love him a lot because he is very special. He probably can't imagine how much I miss his friendship. Finally, now that he's getting old, things won't change. He will always live away at some good friend's house that we will know someday. Always with some new friend who is also a good person. Whenever he visits us with one of them, we laugh. They are always very kind and attentive gentlemen, especially to my two parents.

Now that we're talking about who we like to be with or not, I think about Artur. Apparently, he likes both things: for me to accompany him and for him to come to accompany me. The only problem is that when he comes to Colombia, he never stays with us so that we can enjoy his jokes, and I can laugh when the others laugh because they understood the jokes. That Artur has friends everywhere. They are like the ants in Irina's house in Bradenton, which stick to every crumb they find. In Medellín, he has a friend he likes to accompany all the time. She is already a lady, very beautiful, with big buttocks and breasts. She is the same lady who sometimes lets my other two older brothers accompany her, taking advantage that they come to Medellín from time to time. As for Igor, what can I say? I think he only likes being angry, and my dad keeps waiting for his anger to pass to accompany him a bit and take away his bad mood or for him to accompany my dad and help him find some word in the crossword puzzle that my dad hasn't been able to find.

— *"Ho-o-w a-n-no-ying, Ig-g-o-or-r-rr, bru-u-u-tal! I do-o-on't l-ike hi-im a-a-a-anyth-ii-ingg."*

I feel that Igor never accompanies me, nor do I accompany him. If I'm sure of something, it's that at lunchtime, he likes to accompany my mom so she can serve him a lot. How strange. At that time, he should be accompanying his wife and the children, who surely must be waiting for him to accompany them to eat. I don't know what to think about Boris. He is always at home helping the old people, especially my mom, as my dad doesn't like him accompanying him, nor does he like accompanying him, even for a moment. My father gets very upset when Boris is around. I think my dad doesn't like Boris being at home because he doesn't work and drinks aguardiente all day. My mom, on the other hand, likes him to accompany her because he takes her to the supermarket and sometimes runs errands for her. Boris is very attentive to the two old people. What a pity that he is more interested in the company of bottles than of people. It seems they are in love. As for Raisa, I don't really know. I would say I don't like her accompanying me, nor do I like accompanying her.

I just have to talk a little about Anatoli. At some point, when we visited him in New York, he had a lot of money. However, for several years now, he has stopped talking to my dad and my mom as if he were punishing them for being old. I'll never know what to think. I prefer him as he was so many years ago when he liked me accompanying him, and I liked him accompanying me. It saddens me to know that neither he nor Igor speak to my parents, nor do they speak to me, Irina, Eleonora, or them. However, it's very strange that they haven't spoken to the old people for so long and are here with the family. I've noticed these days that, despite not talking to the old people for so long, they have done it now, although very little. I'll ask Eleonora why they are angry with the old people and with them.

With Mosquitoes and Transparent Lizards

Second time we're going to Mass in Spanish in Miami. This Sunday would be the 7 p.m. Mass at the same church near Eleonora's house. The first time I went, last Sunday, I found it amusing. Especially because they play the guitar and sing beautifully. It reminded me of some hymns from the Church of Santa Gema where my mom takes me every Sunday. Fortunately, they don't play the music that Grandpa the painter liked but the one I like. They sang the way they do in reggaeton and made us applaud while they sang. I don't really like going to Mass, neither here nor in Medellín, because I have to sit and stand up many times.

Mass is hard. Priest says "stand, sit, kneel. Stand, sit, kneel," and when I'm tired of standing up and sitting down, I have to bend my knees and think about the Baby Jesus for a while so they can give me communion that I can't chew, only soften and swallow. My knees hurt a lot when I have to kneel down to think about the Baby Jesus. I've let my mom know that I don't want to go to Mass anymore, but she reminds me that if I don't go, I might get 'it.' My dad doesn't go to Mass because 'it' never happens to him like it does to me.

Maybe it's because he's old and that fades away with time. My mother takes me to Mass so that I don't get 'it,' and if I do, so that I don't get 'it' so often. Since Mass is what protects me from all evil, I prefer to go, even if I don't like it. Many people who go to Mass leave money in the baskets; others go to sleep. Yes..., I've seen them sleeping while everyone stands up and sits down or kneels at the end. The kids who go with their parents take the opportunity to laugh and play quietly, and even to fight while their parents close their eyes to think about the Baby Jesus. The priest giving the Mass was a strange man, with shaved eyebrows. I remember I stared at him for a long time until I couldn't resist anymore and asked Eleonora:

" *Prri-i-ie-e-ess-stt iss Ga-a-ay?*"

My mom heard and elbowed me to shut me up. Another lady nearby must have heard me, and she covered her mouth in shock. The last time my mom elbowed me was at the airport arrival so I would laugh with the policeman. With a confused or embarrassed look, she glanced at Eleonora, who smiled and pretended as if she had heard a joke she couldn't laugh at. That didn't stop me from continuing to look at the priest and thinking he spoke and moved like a woman in a long dress. I kept listening to what I understood from the Mass. Attentive so I could do the same when someone stood up or sat down. My mom taught me that from when I was little. The priest at Santa Gema doesn't look like a woman to me, although he doesn't have a wife or children like Fausto and Boris. That doesn't mean the priest at Santa Gema is gay. Maybe he also has an Amparo to think about. Like me, who is alone, but I think about Amparo. That also means I'm not like the priest in Miami seems to be. Maybe the Baby Jesus doesn't like being disturbed and distracted? Is that why priests don't have wives and little children? Surely neither Fausto nor Boris are gay because if they were, my mom wouldn't like that. I know because she doesn't like blacks or gays at all. I, on the other hand, don't know what to think. The only thing that matters to me is that at least I don't want to be gay, especially now that I only think about Amparo.

When I'm not paying attention to when I should sit or stand up because I'm distracted watching the distracted kids, or the pretty girls from behind, my mom reminds me again with her elbow. She nudges me softly so it doesn't hurt, or so I don't get angry and get 'it' in the middle of Mass. That is, so I realize I should start trying to listen to what the priest is saying. When I go to Mass and the priest is talking, I take the opportunity to remember the things I want. That day I remembered I wanted to eat an ice cream just like the one Camila wanted the day before when I didn't want ice cream but pizza. Surely, if I had preferred ice cream the day before, at Mass I would be thinking I wanted pizza.

I thought about the Baby Jesus as a child, like the picture I have in my wallet. My mom explained to me that when the Baby Jesus grew up, the *Kwai-it Strayn-*

jers came and nailed him to the cross that is in front of the church above where the priest speaks. I still don't know why each church has a different one. There are black ones, white ones, with open and closed eyes, colorful ones, with blood on the knees, with blood on the head or body; some are hung on the cross, some don't have a cross. In short, there are many Baby Jesuses, just like there are many moms and friends of his. I don't understand why there are so many. Maybe it's because there are so many people? When I think about where they make them, I think it's in Miami. I say this because my brother-in-law tells me that in Miami, or Chicago, or New York, they make the Hammer in many colors. They also make Ford, Chevrolet, and others I can't remember. Surely they are different because they make them for blue-eyed people, for brown people, for those who cut the grass in the gardens of Coral Gables, and for people like my mom or like us. Could it be that where people are brown, the Baby Jesus is too? I think so. Now I remember that these days we went to a place to buy toys for Camila. Where the Barbies are displayed. There are Barbies of all colors, and when I asked for the brown Barbies, they told me they were for black people, yes..., for black people, that's what they call brown-skinned people. How weird. Could it be that there are black people inside brown-skinned people?

The Mass started very cheerful, so much so that I thought it would continue that way. When the priest started speaking, many of us began to yawn and compare different people's buttocks. Sometimes, I find some amusing, especially those that are big and saggy. Buttocks are brave because they support us when we're sitting. They are also brave because they endure when the doctor sends injections their way. Amparo has a very nice one, especially when she wears tight pants and walks around the neighborhood. I know many without pants that appear on TV in the early morning. Almost all of them are from girls like Amparo because they only show girls. When I see a pretty girl walking in Miami, I imagine her on TV in the early morning, and I like it, but when I think too much about it, I feel embarrassed and look back at Amparo already wearing pants. How embarrassing for Amparo! Me imagining her without pants. It seems strange to me that when the priest speaks, we all yawn and look at buttocks. The only ones who don't do it are the older ones, again the old ones. Apparently, they are the only ones who pay attention to what's happening. My mom does it too, but my dad doesn't. He just wants to know how to say crossword puzzle words. That day, they told me to ask the Baby Jesus to accompany us on the return trip to Medellín. I did it when it was time to kneel down:

"Ba-a-a-by Je-e-esu-us, he-e-elp the pla-aa-ne a-aarrriiive iiin Me-e-edelli-ín."

I asked for it many times while my stomach was boiling, my throat burning. I wanted lemon, but nobody looked at me, and everyone was kneeling. Every time I have to board a plane, my stomach hurts.

Well, not only when I board a plane. It happened to me when I got lost in Coral Gables or when lightning struck my mom on the head, and they took her to the hospital.

I felt happy when the Mass ended, and the priest gave the blessing. My mom walked out arm in arm with Eleonora. They looked happy to have been together. I don't think Raisa had ever been to Mass. I say this because I had never seen her at Mass. I also noticed she didn't take communion because she sat listening to the songs that some old ladies dressed in purple robes were singing. My mom was the first one to line up for communion, followed by Eleonora and my brother-in-law. Irina didn't take communion either. Nor did the men who accompanied us. Apparently, only my mother, Eleonora, my brother-in-law, and I believed in Baby Jesus, and the others were just there to accompany us. We returned home in several cars, the same groups that had arrived. For the past two days, Eleonora has made it clear to me that I should pack my suitcase for when they announce the return to Medellín. From what I've heard, it will be in the next few days.

It seems I have to start saving all the car catalogs I've collected in the places my brother-in-law has taken me. Although I still can't pronounce 'l-a-m-b-o-r-g-h-i-n-i,' I already have fourteen pictures my brother-in-law took of me in various orange and yellow ones, in the place where they sell them. Riding in that car was very nice. In Medellín, there are none. I haven't seen them yet because there are only Hammers that come to Comuna Trece. Hugo will be very happy to see me riding in those cars, and surely, someday, he'll want to come to Miami to ride them too. For now, I'll lend him my photos so he won't feel like coming. Anyway, he can't do it because his mom never takes him to places other than Medellín. Is it because his mom lives in the United States and he never sees her?

These days were filled with shopping. Everyone wanted to buy. They bought three flat-screen TVs to replace the big ones still in our rooms that people can't see well anymore. They also bought sneakers for everyone. Some light brown ones so my mom's ankles wouldn't hurt while she stood cooking in the kitchen, and black ones that can be bent by hand, supposedly so my dad can walk around the Laureles neighborhood every day and not get tired. Others for Raisa, the color of flamingos, those birds I saw at the zoo and that remind me of Amparo. She bought them supposedly because they are cheaper than in London and because they are also prettier than the ones there. Also, supposedly to go to the gym every day at seven in the morning. From what I see, Raisa had many reasons to buy those flamingo sneakers. They also bought white sneakers for Boris. Boris didn't buy them; it was my old Anastasia, my mom, who really likes Boris despite my dad blaming her for everything she does related to him. It seems to me that Boris is a sad brother, even though he doesn't seem like it. He's getting old and doesn't have friends, neither male nor female. All old people like Boris have children, or at least they've had a girlfriend or a wife. But not him... at least as far as I remember or know. I feel a bit sorry for him because, like me, he can only see through one eye, and although he has two, only one works. His left eye works, and mine only works on the right side. We never talk about our things at home, that is, about all the things that happen to us, although we all know. For example, I know what happened to Boris's eye when it was good. We know this in my house because we've known each other forever... but we never talk about it, especially not me, because I wouldn't know how to talk about things properly.

Boris is going through the same thing I am, except that with his good eye, he can see in all directions. In contrast, I can only see straight ahead. I know that because my mother has explained it to me for years, and I've tried very hard to understand. I think I know what I'm talking about. I've talked about this before.

What I can tell you about Boris's lost eye is that when he was little and went to elementary school, he stuck a pencil in it. I don't know if he fell with the pencil in his hand, or if a friend wanted to take it from him, or if he wanted to take it from a friend. What a pity... later, when he was older, around fourteen, when I was very small and always accompanied Boris, my dad, Igor, Artur, and Anatoli to play billiards and drink beer or aguardiente, Boris started drinking aguardiente and beer too, and he hasn't been able to stop since. That's what saddens me the most. One-eyed, drunk, alone, and with a dad who doesn't care about him at all. Boris smells strongly of cigarettes and spends his time talking on the phone, saying vulgarities and bossing many people around. In short, the white shoes my mom bought him will probably be for him to wear on Sundays, because during the week, he only wears black or brown shoes.

Speaking of shopping, neither Eleonora, Irina, Artur, nor Fausto bought sneakers for themselves, maybe because they live here in Miami and can buy them whenever they want. One thing they all did was buy clothes. They even bought for me. Eleonora kept her promise and bought me a new video game console. She had promised it to me. By now, I had played it several times and had learned something. I really like playing the latest games that have come out, no matter how difficult they are. Eduardito, my little nephew, tried to teach me how to play golf in a video game they gave him, but I couldn't learn. I see the ball too small, and every time I swing the club, I can't hit it, so he has to do it for me. Eduardito also taught me to make cakes in another video game. I liked doing that, but I won't play it because only girls play dressing up dolls. I wonder if the priest in Miami plays with dolls on the video game console? It's possible, but I don't think the priest of Santa Gema does it because he doesn't resemble the priest here.

That night, when we returned from Mass, we gathered in the dining room. We were hungry, and although the food wasn't ready yet, the women, except for Raisa, started preparing something quick that would keep us away from hunger for at least a couple of hours. Despite the hunger that was plaguing us, we were still having a very special time because everyone was smiling. Even Anatoli and Igor, who no longer laughed as they did when they were young and hadn't yet married or had my nephews who are now grown and already married. Anatoli doesn't laugh anymore. I haven't seen him laugh for a long time. He's always serious, adding things on a calculator he never puts down. He prefers reading and reading rather than laughing. Now that I think about it, he's a bit like me because that's how I stay. Maybe that's why we're brothers. I have the impression that he keeps many things in his head. Everyone in my house says Anatoli is crazy. I don't know if they say it for real or in jest, making fun of him. Maybe it's true because he doesn't talk to my parents, and only crazy people do that. They say he's been crazy for a long time and that he's only interested in money. They also say he only likes to talk about money and that's why he married Irma Lomanto, a very dear lady who apparently has a lot of money and works taking care of the money for a man who also has a lot of money. More money than she does and all my brothers and friends put together. In other words, he has many banks and supermarkets where they sell money to people like my dad who always goes to buy it when he runs out of what he has in his pocket. Maybe that's why when I have to refer to Anatoli, I always say:

"Ah-nah-toh-lee h-has ah l-lot of m-muh-nee."

The day's shopping was still scattered all over the place, and Eleonora's house looked more like a store than a home. Seeing it all like that made me sad once again. I couldn't help it. I think I was already used to having them close, and for sure, when we left again, we would be far away and lonelier than ever. Once again, I stopped eating and felt a burning sensation in my stomach. I went to the fridge and took out a lemon that I cut and drank its juice. However, my stomach burned even more. Eleonora came to help me. I don't know how she finds out that I need help. That's my mom. She appears when I need her to appear. That time Eleonora gave me flaxseed water that she always keeps fresh. That helped me.

I went back to the window of the house facing the street, allowing me to see other houses' gardens. I stayed there for a long time while everyone at the table talked and the kids slept. I thought about my old mom, about me not being as old as them, but not as young either, and I thought about my dad. I thought he couldn't be so attentive to me anymore, and I hurried. I thought about asking my dad to buy another woman, younger, or talk to Eleonora to live with us in Medellín.

I felt the laughter of Artur, Eleonora, and Boris, who were the loudest. I would have liked to be understanding their jokes once again, like when I wanted to understand everything they talked about or said. I would have liked to have known everything related to the old piece of furniture and other things I would like to comprehend. But those were just things I noticed, even when the table was gradually emptying, and the night made everything quieter. The cars hardly passed in front of the house anymore, and only the neighborhood lights made the gardens noticeable.

I focused on watching the mosquitoes flying around the lamp and the white lizards eating them. It was very fun to see how the lizards come out all white at night. That is, pale, almost transparent. My brother-in-law explained to me that they are the same lizards from the day, but at night, they change color so mosquitoes won't notice them so much and let themselves be eaten. Despite the lizards and the mosquitoes distracting me, I still felt very sad. Maybe because inside me, I saw my mom very old, or because I felt I would miss them all when we returned to Medellín. That's when I felt my brother-in-law put his hand on my shoulder. I smiled at him, but I still didn't want to tell him about my sadness. Perhaps he had already noticed it in my disobedient eyes. He asked me if I wasn't sleepy. I told him no. I told him about the lizards and the mosquitoes, and he smiled. I think he understood it was better to leave me alone, and he left. He would go to bed like the others. Eleonora also approached me a few minutes later. She kissed me and asked me to go to bed early. I assured her I would, although I knew it was a lie. I never sleep before three in the morning, and that sad night would be longer for me because nothing I was thinking about was happy. Not even when I thought about Amparo because I saw her with her boyfriends or friends hugging her and giving her kisses while I was watching her up close. I thought about Hugo, and I was also sad. Just imagining that he doesn't have his mom near him makes me sad. I think he should get another mom who would be close to him. If my mom weren't so old, I would ask her to be Hugo's mom; he would be a very good brother to me. That's right; I'll ask my mom to exchange Anatoli, who doesn't talk to her, or even Igor, for Hugo. Can you imagine Anatoli and Igor being children of a mom who doesn't love them and has never been with them?

Thinking about Hugo, I realized that only he could tell me how it feels to live without a mom. Yes, that's it. He can let me know what to do when my mom dies of old age or from a heart attack, or because a bullet in Medellín kills her, without even knowing where it came from. I'll ask him if he felt like crying when he found out his mom wasn't with him because she went to New York. That way, I'll know if I'll cry when they finally decide to throw my mom in the trash, as I believe they do very often with the old people in Bradenton.

Alone, with the lizards and mosquitoes, I started to think about the people I know who don't have a mom. I thought about my brother-in-law. I remember asking him if he was very sad about his mom's death, and he said yes. He also said that, on the other hand, he felt happy about her death because she was very ill and her death meant she had stopped suffering. He explained that stopping suffering means not feeling any more *ayayay*. He told me that with her death, his mom's headaches wouldn't bother her anymore, referring to the *ayayay*. I understood everything he explained about the sadness and joy one feels when old people die. I felt fear because my mom gets those lightning bolts in her head, and that's why they take her to the hospital. I also assumed that if she dies because of those lightning bolts, then those bolts wouldn't cause her any more pain, and I felt a bit happy, although not entirely. What a pity that she also has to die so that she doesn't suffer anymore. I felt anxious for her, and I hurried to Eleonora's bed, who already had her arms covered with a blanket. I touched her shoulder, and she uncovered herself.

"What's wrong, baby?" she asked me, a little frightened.

"I'm s-sad, s-sad."

"Sad about what, baby?" she said, sitting up in bed.

"M-mom's too old... She d-died, hea-ad hurts, ayayay. I'm s-sad, s-sad."

She hugged me affectionately. My brother-in-law woke up too, but she said something to him, and he went back to bed. Then she took my hand and led me to the living room, where the sofa was where I was supposed to sleep. She sat down and hugged me. Then she said:

"Sad, sad, not baby... I love you very much!"

And she hugged me tightly again and almost didn't let go. In fact, I almost didn't let her go. I wished she would never let me go. As far as I can remember, my mom stopped hugging me when I started to grow up and become more argumentative. I preferred her not to hug me anymore because I didn't like it. I was very evasive and rude. I still am. Poor old lady, she's had it tough. Now I wish she would hug me like Eleonora did, but I feel like she's lost the habit. Maybe she doesn't do it because she's afraid. She probably thinks I'll say something stupid and insult her. She's always been with me, but not that close. My dad is the same way. He comes close, puts his hand on my shoulder, and pats me only on our birthdays. When it's our birthdays or their birthdays, after saying "happy birthday" to each other, the three of us go to a restaurant to eat whatever each of us wants. Just the three of us because my brothers just call on the phone that day. Something I know happens every year on our birthdays is that Eleonora calls all my brothers to remind them to congratulate us. To congratulate us, because they almost never remember. In other words, they almost never remember the old folks.

To finish this about hugs, I can say that in my house in Medellín, the little candles lit on the cakes, like before, have disappeared. When the joy of everyone in the house was the most important thing. Joy also left our house; it moved to where the neighbors or the friends from the neighborhood live. What I mean is that hugs are scarce in my house. The one who always hugs me when she sees me around is Eleonora. She's very cool. She's not afraid that I'll reject her or if she is, she pretends not to be because she knows I like her hugs. Amparo has never really hugged me, I mean, when I visit her for real. We hug when I see her in movies or magazines or imagine her transformed into one of those women I've seen on the boats where we went for a ride these days with everyone who is in Miami visiting Eleonora.

Tonight, I wanted to cry a lot, and I did. I cried a part of it while Eleonora hugged me and rubbed my back. During this trip to Miami, I've received more hugs than in all my years of living alone with my parents. They hugged me when I arrived, when I got lost in Coral Gables and then reappeared, and when I cried hugging Eleonora. To make me stop crying, she said the same thing she says when I'm sad thinking about what will become of me when my parents die. First, she said that she loves me very much and also that my parents will never die because they will always stay in my head, smiling. I felt a bit better, although only as long as she was with me. She offered me a glass of milk and a cake they had prepared in the afternoon. One of those delicious cakes my mom makes when she invites her friends to have coffee and talk all afternoon about the same things they talk about every afternoon when they invite each other to eat cake with coffee.

Again, I was left alone with the transparent lizards and the foolish mosquitoes that, for not paying attention, let themselves be eaten. This time, after a while, we weren't so alone because, hopping, a horrible toad with wrinkled skin, big, half black and half brown, approached the light as if nothing was happening.

It walked discreetly instead of jumping, and after adjusting itself, it started sticking out its tongue and eating mosquitoes that stood under the streetlight. I really liked seeing it; I had only seen them eat on television before. I saw it for real, how they eat flies, crickets, or cockroaches. They do it with their tongues. It was very funny for me to see it for real. There were already many of us who stayed awake at that time of night. There were many toads, many lizards, and not so many mosquitoes. After a few hours, I felt my stomach rumbling as it does every night when I'm still awake, watching television or thinking without watching television. I knew it was time to close my window. I wanted to rest, but not before making myself some cold oatmeal in the blender, with lots of milk and sugar. What a pity that Camila cried when the blender was making the oatmeal. She cried for a few minutes, but then stopped. I sat down to have the oatmeal at the dining table in the dark, and I noticed my dad going to the bathroom and then Irina. My mom did too, and then everyone. The only ones who didn't were my nephew Eduardito and my brother-in-law. It seemed like everyone had been watching white lizards and mosquitoes, and like me, they couldn't sleep because they were sad. Anyway, I tried to sleep. It was already three in the morning or something like that. It was strange because, due to watching white lizards, toads, and mosquitoes, I didn't watch television or think about Amparo. In my bed, I found myself lost in thought, as I usually do when I'm lost in thought. Talking to myself as always when I talk to myself. Imagining myself looking and looking like when I imagine looking and looking. Glued to my little window from where I usually look. One more night. This time, everyone was asleep, despite Artur's chilling snores. I think I'll close my little window. I'm tired of trying to see everything, and I have to sleep.

—... *Uu-u-ntil to-m-mo-o-rrow, dea-a-r Ampa-a-aro-o.*

For the Return

"Wha-at the hee-ellll?" I exclaimed.

It was all I could say when the plane touched down in Medellín and shook as if it was falling apart, rolling and rolling, very, very fast on that ground; fighting against that harassing wind, angry because the plane had arrived without asking for permission and without wanting to stop. And we, in that plane, making an effort to help it not go so fast or to go slower and slower against that wind that sounded and screamed furiously because the plane wanted to beat it.

Oh... I felt a strong urge to pee, so I clenched my buttocks to avoid it, just as my old lady tells me to do when I want to pee and can't because I'm far from a bathroom... and I kept anxious, feeling the plane that couldn't stop because it beat the wind, and I started to sweat and sweat and I looked at my mother, and she looked at me terrified, hoping that I wouldn't get scared because I might do that stupid thing I do when I get scared.

And although that beast is getting weaker because the wind has started to win, I keep sweating for a while, and my armpits itch, and I have to scratch until I also feel lighter, with less weight on my neck. And even though I don't sweat much because I don't even sweat or only a little when I'm overheated from the beating I took in Coral Gables or because of that nonsense thing I get when things aren't how I want them, and I lose control, and it only goes away when I go see the Baby Jesus in the church in Miami or at Santa Gema, and I start to feel like the plane and like the wind that, tired of fighting so much between them, don't want to make so much effort anymore, and both think they have won.

Uff... Now everything is calmer because the wind and the plane have quieted down, and people don't seem scared, and my mother keeps looking at me, and I see her with a smile in her eyes, as if to say...

"Stay calm, son, we are still alive."

We arrived in Medellín a few minutes before one on my watch...

Walking through the airport corridor in search of the exit, my head saw Amparo running to greet me very quickly, just like how girlfriends greet boyfriends when they haven't seen each other in many months and really want to see each other. I watched her run toward me very quickly, but slowly, like they run in movies when it seems they're going very fast, but they're actually running floating, and their hair floats, and their skirts float, and their breasts float, and their face, and their buttocks, and their hands, and their gaze, and her... And seeing me, she shows her happy teeth that come out of her mouth because they want to fly to reach me first, because she sent me a smile first, before her eyes looked at me anxiously because they didn't want to be beaten by the teeth either. Her gaze wanted to reach me before her smile. Here comes Amparo, coming towards me, painted like a flamingo. She's not painted like a flamingo. She is a flamingo that makes her boyfriends sad because they pursue her but can't catch her, that also makes her sister angry because she decided not to love her anymore because she behaves badly with me and because she only wants to hug me, touch me, ask me, "How was Miami, Ludovico?" Like those girlfriends who run across the fields to hug their boyfriends who return from war, dressed as soldiers, happy because nothing happened to them there.

"Ludovico, help your dad with the suitcase, he's very tired..." my old lady says.

"Ah-h-h? Wha-a-a-at?"

"The suitcase," my mother says, pointing.

"Whi-i-i-ich o-o-o-ne?" I stammered, feeling embarrassed. I couldn't understand her because at that very moment, Amparo was about to hug me.

"Whi-i-i-ich o-o-o-ne?" I asked again.

END

Ludovico

Also from
William Castano-Bedoya

WE THE OTHER PEOPLE: THE BEGGARS OF THE MERCURY LIGHTS
(2023 · English and Spanish Versions Available)

We the Other People -The Beggars of the Mercury Lights- introduces a new voice in American social literature, narrating the relationship between political power and invisible poverty amidst a crisis of conservative values, social injustice, the excesses of extremism, and the politicization of human suffering as a tool of power in the United States.

The story focuses on a family, the Newmans, whose recent economic misfortune has plunged their patriarch into a depressive state in the years leading up to the global health crisis, which forms the backdrop of the novel. Steve Newman struggles to overcome his condition, creating imaginary games in which he blends experiences and fiction as therapy to ward off depression. From his misfortune and desperation emerges the resilience that rescues him from the demons that haunt him, turning him into a more compassionate member of society. Steve must come to terms with his new life, no longer from the height of opulence as he did before his failure, but now knowing firsthand society's abandonment of the poor and the socially 'invisible.' Castaño-Bedoya's novel recreates the lives of those who endure the difficulties of existence under the failure of the Constitution, and who clamor for their universal right to live without fear.

WE'LL MEET IN STOCKHOLM
(2024 · English and Spanish Versions Available)

"Being a novelist is less important than living to be one." In the vibrant backdrop of New Orleans' bohemian French Quarter, six independent writers convene at La apassion for writing, they inhabit an old house where they confront the harsh realities of an ever-evolving publishing industry. In this atmosphere of camaraderie and competition, literary aspirations intertwine with the complexities of human relationships.

The novel "We'll meet in Stockholm" pays homage to these courageous writers who strive to be heard in a world often indifferent to their talents. Laden with sarcasm, the title reflects the distant aspiration of winning the coveted Nobel Prize in Literature. For these writers, Stockholm embodies both an ironic utopia and a symbol of La Tertulia's unyielding spirit. Through their intertwined stories, "We'll meet in Stockholm" delves into the complexity of the creative process, friendship, and the sacrifices necessary to pursue a shared passion. It is an exhilarating journey through the heart of creativity, where hope and irony intertwine in the eternal quest for literary greatness.

"FLOWERS FOR MARIA SUCEL"
(2006/2013/2021 & 2022 · English and Spanish Versions Available).

Exile isn't always physical. In this saga of love, courage, and brokenness, the author reflects on the journey of a suddenly impoverished family as they struggle to survive migration to a cold, uncaring third-world capital. Trying desperately to keep body and soul together, its members are torn apart by their inner exiles: A woman bearing child after child in silent submission to tradition. Children bewildered and detached by constant upheaval. A father's secret life and the bitter ostracism that turns him into a lonely stranger under the family roof. In Flowers for María Sucel, love is a fragile yet enduring thing that blooms when least expected.

THE GALPON
(2023 · English and Spanish Versions Available)

When the human condition is what directly induces the success or failure of a human being's endeavor, whoever does not evolve goes backwards... Likewise, although supposedly frivolous freedom is currently what governs the global market, its results are ultimately the consequence of man's influence. This is the essence of the corporate world, as William Castaño-Bedoya puts it, in a novel with characters more loyal to profit and fundamentalism than their colleagues and employees. HanssenBox allows itself to wander, led by what its leaders see as destiny, at a time when technology and the online commercial market become industry titans.

Ethan, the company's life manager, and Oliver, an outside consultant, star in that microcosm in a corner of the southeastern United States. The two work under the command of a businessman with a shady disposition who plunges them into episodes of mutual distrust, egocentrism, and insecurity. The lives of the characters are systematically affected by the weight of extremist ideologies and the omnipresence of an underhanded double standard . HanssenBox floats along the passage of circumstances imposed by fate in an era in which e-commerce undertakes a crushing advance without return.

www.ingramcontent.com/pod-product-compliance
Lightning Source LLC
Chambersburg PA
CBHW031040160726
47991CB00005B/1961